A REAL CHRISTIAN

A REAL CHRISTIAN

THE LIFE OF
JOHN WESLEY

Kenneth J. Collins

ABINGDON PRESS
Nashville

A REAL CHRISTIAN: THE LIFE OF JOHN WESLEY

Copyright © 1999 by Abingdon Press

This book is printed on elemental chlorine–free paper.

Library of Congress Cataloging-in-Publication Data

Collins, Kenneth J.
    A real Christian : the life of John Wesley / Kenneth J. Collins.
      p. cm.
    Includes bibliographical references and index.
    ISBN 0-687-08246-3 (alk. paper)
    1. Wesley, John, 1703–1791. 2. Methodist Church—England—Clergy—Biography.
I. Title.
    BX8495.W5C754 1999
287'.092—dc21
[B]   99-10346
                                          CIP

Scripture quotations noted NRSV are from the New Revised Standard Version Bible, copyright © 1989, by the Division of Christian Education of the National Council of the Churches of Christ in the United States of America. Used by permission.

Other quotations are from the Authorized or King James Version of the Bible.

03 04 05 06 07 08—10 9 8 7 6 5

MANUFACTURED IN THE UNITED STATES OF AMERICA

For Richard P. Heitzenrater, the mentor of us all,
with appreciation

I would like to express sincere thanks to Dr. Richard Heitzenrater of Duke Divinity School and to Dr. Bill Kostlevy of Asbury Theological Seminary who read the manuscript in its early stages and offered many helpful comments.

CONTENTS

1

The Family Circle

Samuel Wesley was born at Whitchurch in 1662, the year in which the Church of England enforced the Act of Uniformity and thereby required the use of the Book of Common Prayer in all her parishes. Compelled by conscience and by Puritan sensibilities, both Samuel's father and grandfather lost their positions in the church during Bartholomew-tide of that year.

Growing up in a dissenting home, Samuel was serious, devout, and keenly interested in religious affairs. Like many other children of dissent, he was educated at the Free School, Dorchester, until he was fifteen. While still a boy, however, Samuel rejected the Puritan heritage of his family, having considered these matters very carefully, and in 1683 made his way to Oxford and enrolled at Exeter College as a servitor—a poor scholar who would meet his costs, in part, by serving older students. A good student with a scholarly bent, Samuel received his bachelor of arts degree in June 1688, and his masters degree from Cambridge in 1694. His acceptance into the Anglican Church was reaffirmed, and his gifts and graces for ministry were acknowledged in his ordination to deacon in 1688, by Dr. Sprat, Bishop of Rochester, and to the priesthood in 1689 by Dr. Compton, the Bishop of London.

As a young man, in 1682 Samuel Wesley had the good fortune to meet Susanna Annesley, perhaps for the first time at the wedding of Susanna's sister to John Dunton, the noted bookseller. That Samuel and Susanna themselves would eventually marry comes as no surprise when we consider their similar background and interests. Like Samuel, Susanna was raised in a dissenting home. Her father, Samuel Annesley, was a principal leader of the Nonconformists and was Vicar of St. Giles, Cripplegate, until he was ejected in 1662. Like Samuel, Susanna decided, as a youth, to make her way back to the Anglican Church to the chagrin of her family. And like Samuel, Susanna was both pious and disciplined, giving herself only "as much time for recreation as [she] spent in private devotion."[1]

In 1691, shortly after their marriage, Samuel and Susanna moved to the rectory at South Ormsby in Lincolnshire, a position secured for them through the good graces of the Marquis of Normanby. During this period Samuel added to his meager income by publishing in the *Athenian Gazette* and elsewhere. Around 1696 or so, the Wesleys moved from South Ormsby to Epworth in Lincolnshire where Samuel served as rector. There is evidence that Samuel believed he had received this appointment at the request of Queen Mary herself in appreciation for a work that he had published in defense of the Glorious Revolution. However, since Queen Mary died in 1694, nearly two years before the appointment at Epworth, the queen must have expressed her intention on this matter shortly before her demise—if Samuel's reckoning was indeed correct.

At any rate, Samuel, who was a Tory in politics, not only affirmed the divine right of monarchs, but believed, as we have just seen, in the legitimacy of the rule of William of Orange and of his queen, Mary, the daughter of James II of England. Samuel's young wife, however, of equally strong convictions, was a Jacobite at heart and held that James II and his son James III and not King William were the lawful rulers of England. One evening in 1702, Samuel observed that Susanna had not said "Amen" to his prayer for the king. Such silence roiled Samuel, and upon learning of Susanna's Jacobite sympathies he rashly vowed, "Sukey, if that be the case, we must part, for if we have two Kings, we must have two beds."[2] With the kind of stubbornness that emerges only from a deeply principled person, Samuel abandoned his wife and children and headed for London. For how long Samuel forsook his family is a point well disputed, but what is clear is that the neglectful husband and father eventually returned to the Epworth rectory without having received the assurances from Susanna that he had demanded in his vow. On June 17 (28), 1703,[3] within a year of Samuel's return, John Wesley was born.

The Wesley family was large, even by eighteenth-century standards, and consisted of nineteen children, of whom John was the fifteenth. Unfortunately, due to the poor medical practices of the day, of these many children nine died as infants. Given such circumstances, Samuel was often hard-pressed to support his family from the modest salary at Epworth and from what little money he could garner from his writings. Moreover, his inability to handle what money he had—evident on numerous occasions—complicated matters, and so Samuel was frequently in debt. During the local elections of 1705, for example, he came out forcefully for certain candidates. Upon learning more about their actual positions, the Epworth rector quickly and publicly changed his mind. Such a reversal of support sparked the ire of several people in Epworth, and one of Samuel's parishioners, to get even, called in a loan that Samuel was unable to repay. Soon he was arrested and placed in the debtor's prison at Lincoln Castle.

With her economic condition uncertain, Susanna had good cause for concern. Fortunately, Archbishop Sharpe, in many ways a kind and generous man, rallied support among the clergy on Samuel's behalf and eventually paid off his immediate debts. During Samuel's imprisonment, the archbishop had visited Susanna at the rectory and asked whether her situation were so bad that "she had ever wanted bread." Susanna replied forthrightly and in a way that epitomized her condition at Epworth: "My Lord, I will freely own to your Grace, that strictly speaking, I never did want bread. But then, I had so much care to get it, before it was eat, and to pay for it after, as has often made it very unpleasant to me."[4]

With her husband occasionally gone at Convocation, and with several children clamoring for her attention, Susanna had many opportunities to exercise strong leadership in the family. Something of a disciplinarian, she cared for her children according to rule and method. All of the Wesley children, for instance, except Kezzy, were taught to read when they were five years old, and a single day was allotted to the task of learning the alphabet, a task John and others accomplished quite easily though Mary and Anne took a day and a half. Moreover, on each day of the week, Susanna had a private talk with one of her children according to a fixed pattern: on Monday with Mollie, on Tuesday with Hetty, on Wednesday with Nancy, on Thursday with John, on Friday with

Patty, on Saturday with Charles, and on Sunday with Emilia and Sukey.[5] Six hours a day were spent at school where instruction was serious and thorough and where loud talking and boisterous playing were strictly forbidden.

Reflecting in his later years, John Wesley was so impressed with his mother's educational practices that he asked her to collect the principal rules she had practiced in their family. In a letter to her son on July 24, 1732, Susanna detailed her method and underscored that element which is absolutely necessary for the inculcation of piety and for the proper foundation of a religious education:

> In order to form the minds of children, the first thing to be done is to conquer their will.... I insist upon conquering the wills of children betimes, because this is the only foundation for a religious education. When this is thoroughly done, then a child is capable of being governed by the reason of its parent, till its own understanding comes to maturity.[6]

In addition, Susanna listed the various "bylaws" which were a part of the Epworth household:

1. Whoever was charged with a fault, of which they were guilty, if they would ingenuously confess it, and promise to amend, should not be beaten. This rule prevented a great deal of lying.

2. That no sinful action, as lying, pilfering, playing at church, or on the Lord's day, disobedience, quarreling, etc., should ever pass unpunished.

3. That no child should ever be chid or beat twice for the same fault.

4. That every signal act of obedience...should be always commended, and frequently rewarded, according to the merits of the cause.

5. That if ever any child performed an act of obedience, or did anything with an intention to please, though the performance was not well, yet the obedience and intention should be kindly accepted, and the child with sweetness directed how to do better for the future.

6. That propriety be inviolably preserved, and none suffered to invade the property of another in the smallest matter, though it were but of the value of a farthing, or a pin.

7. That promises be strictly observed; and a gift once bestowed, and so the right passed away from the donor, be not resumed.

8. That no girl be taught to work till she can read very well; and then that she be kept to her work with the same application, and for the same time, that she was held to in reading. This rule also is much to be observed; for the putting children to learn sewing before they can read perfectly is the very reason why so few women can read fit to be heard, and never to be well understood.[7]

In light of such precepts, modern writers have often criticized Susanna's educational practices as unduly harsh and rigorous. But John Wesley, himself, evidently did not think so. In fact, in his later years Wesley repeatedly cautioned against the unholy triumvirate of "pride, self-will, and love of the world," especially in his sermons, as well as against the pernicious nature of self-will in particular, that desire to live according to human autonomy where one's own will and desires, rather than the gracious and loving will of God, become the chief guides of life.

Despite this regularity of discipline, the home life of the Wesley family was disrupted from time to time by unusual events. In 1701, for example, their barn—though reputedly well constructed—simply collapsed. The next year part of the rectory was burned, and in 1704 fire destroyed all the flax that had been planted to ease the financial burden of the family. The most noteworthy of these unusual events, however, and the most dangerous of all, was the fire that swept through the Epworth rectory on February 9, 1709. At midnight, Samuel was awakened by a cry from the street, "Fire!" He opened his bedroom door and found the house filled with smoke. After waking Susanna and his two eldest daughters, Samuel raced for the nursery where the maid was sleeping with five children. Startled by his entrance and smelling the smoke, the maid grabbed the youngest child, Charles, and urged the others to follow her lead. The three older children did so, but John remained fast asleep.

Most of the family gathered outside the rapidly burning rectory. Some children had escaped through windows, others through a small door that led to the garden, but John was nowhere to be seen. Thinking it was morning due to the light from the blaze, John finally awoke and called out for the maid. His cries were heard from the street, and Samuel darted back into the house and attempted to mount the burning stairs, which quickly gave way under his weight. Fearing John was lost, Samuel knelt down in the hall and commended his soul to God. Meanwhile, seeing the flames lick the ceiling of his room, John attempted to flee through a doorway, but found it impossible. He then climbed onto a chest near the window and was spotted by those in the yard. A ladder was called for. One man stood on top of the shoulders of another and reached for the child. At the very moment John Wesley was in his rescuer's arms, the roof came crashing down and fell inward, sending debris, smoke, and flames into the night sky. With this turn of events, Samuel cried out with a sense of relief: "Come, neighbours, let us kneel down: let us give thanks to God! he has given me all my eight children: let the house go, I am rich enough."[8]

Though John was to remember these events well, it was Susanna Wesley who first clearly discerned the providential care of God in the deliverance of February 9. Thus, shortly after the fire she professed: "I do intend to be more particularly careful of the soul of this child, that thou hast so mercifully provided for, than ever I have been, that I may do my endeavor to instill into his mind the principles of thy *true* religion and virtue."[9] In a similar fashion, the fire revealed to John Wesley not only God's superintending providence, but also that the Lord had perhaps a special plan, a noble purpose, for his life. Such thoughts emboldened and invigorated John with a strong sense of mission early in life. In fact, at one point he had an emblem of a house in flames placed under one of his portraits with a caption that read: "Is not this a brand plucked out of the burning" (Zech. 3:2), though later he added a disclaimer about all of this.

To be sure, there has been much speculation by Wesley's biographers, both past and present, about the cause of the inferno on February 9—the chief suspicion being arson by malicious neighbors—but there is little that can be affirmed with certainty. What is clear is that Samuel had irritated many of the inhabitants on the island of Axholme, where Epworth was situated, by calling for the draining of the marshes, an act that many believed would undermine their livelihood. Fifty years earlier, the people of Epworth had tried to stifle the efforts of the Dutch engineer Cornelius Vermuyden—whom William of Orange had sent to drain the land—by burning his crops, beating his workers, and breaking down the dams he had built. Such animosity, in other words, had a history, and it led John Wesley, at least, to surmise in later life that the fire had been deliberately set by his neighbors. But we will never know for sure. Indeed, some historians conjecture that the fire may have been due to "a certain carelessness on the part of the Rector."[10]

In any case, many of Samuel's relationships, both near and far, were strained to say the least, due chiefly to his strongly held opinions and to his frequent indebtedness. For example, his own curate, Mr. Inman, who preached on occasion during Samuel's absence at Convocation, refused to depart from the well-worn topic that Christians ought to pay their debts. Whether the text was Romans 1:19 or Matthew 5:19 made little difference; the message was the same: pay your debts. Was it, then, that the rector of Epworth had owed his curate some money? And was this curate intent on embarrassing the rector until he got it? So matters stood when in 1712 Samuel again asked Inman to assume the responsibilities of the Epworth parish. Not surprisingly, the dull curate sallied forth with yet another harangue on the obligation of Christians to pay their debts. Susanna, sensing the displeasure of the congregation as well as the absence of sound spiritual care, decided to begin holding evening services in her kitchen (which started out as prayers for her family, and soon after many neighbors asked if they could participate) in order to minister to the needs of the people. In these services, which were well attended, psalms were sung, prayers were read, and a sermon drawn from Samuel's library shelves was recited by Susanna to the edification of all. Inman, chafing under Susanna's able and steady leadership, especially since her evening services were better attended than his morning ones, wrote a letter to Samuel and complained bitterly about Susanna's inappropriate actions.

Conventional in many respects, and concerned with good order, Samuel asked his wife to end these informal gatherings which so inflamed his curate. Susanna, not easily dissuaded in anything, considered the matter carefully and responded to her husband's request by engaging in some serious theological reflection—reflection that Samuel, himself, ultimately found convincing. Susanna wrote:

> If you do, after all, think fit to dissolve this assembly, do not tell me that you desire me to do it, for that will not satisfy my conscience; but send me your positive command, in such full and express terms as may absolve me from all guilt and punishment, for neglecting this opportunity of doing good, when you and I shall appear before the great and awful tribunal of our LORD JESUS CHRIST.[11]

If Samuel was concerned about the spiritual state of the Epworth congregation, if he was strong-willed in religious matters, and if he was deeply marked by convictions, for which he was willing to suffer, then so too was Susanna. Indeed, on matters of principle, especially in the area of religion, Susanna was as firm and as resolute as her husband. These two earnest and sincere people, these strong personalities, together provided an atmosphere in the Epworth rectory that would instill an uncanny seriousness in moral and spiritual affairs in many of their children with the good result that all three of their sons—Samuel, Jr., John, and Charles—would eventually become priests of the Church of England.

Though the influence of the Epworth rectory on the Wesley children in the form of lessons, prayers, and parental discipline is clear, we must also remember that in the case of John Wesley, as with his brother Charles, such influence was relatively short-lived. Nominated for the Charterhouse School in London by the Duke of Buckingham, John matriculated at this institution—once a Carthusian monastery—as a gown-boy in January 1714 when he was but ten-and-a-half years old. A favorite of Thomas Walker, the School Master, John Wesley was well liked at the school though he had to suffer, from time to time, the same indignities that all the younger students experienced at the hands of the older ones. In one practice, the boys of the higher classes took the portion of meat meant for the younger ones. Having a lean diet, and taking the advice of his father to run around the Charterhouse courtyard three times a day, young John Wesley was no doubt in good physical condition at the time.

When Wesley was in his mid thirties he would recall the days of a relatively carefree youth at Charterhouse, of a boy who was presumptuously satisfied with his own religious life. For example, in an autobiographical narrative which precedes his Aldersgate account of May 24, 1738, Wesley observed:

> The next six or seven years were spent at school, where outward restraints being removed, I was much more negligent than before even of outward duties, and almost continually guilty of outward sins, which I knew to be such, though they were not scandalous in the eye of the world. However, I still read the Scriptures, and said my prayers, morning and evening: And what I now hoped to be saved by, was, (1) not being so bad as other people; (2) having still a kindness for religion; and (3) reading the Bible, going to church, and saying my prayers.[12]

This is a revealing narrative. Although it clearly represents the perspective of a man looking back on his youth—and is no doubt colored by that later vantage point—it nevertheless displays the same kind of sensitivity and religious judgment of a Luther in the sixteenth century or of a Kierkegaard in the nineteenth. Like Luther who preceded him, Wesley's conscience was not easily put aside, and he was hardly satisfied with the conventional religion of his Charterhouse days. Indeed, the round of religious duties, which included the means of grace, left him simply with a "kindness for religion." And though the young Wesley was clearly not plagued by the overbearing scruples of the monastic Luther, the older Wesley began to evidence pangs of conscience that others hardly or rarely felt. Moreover, like Kierkegaard who followed him, Wesley was a perplexing, even mysterious, figure because he doubted and called into question precisely what others so readily assumed: namely, what it means to be a Christian. For one thing, why was Wesley in retrospect not satisfied with the religious staples of his life at Charterhouse—such as praying, reading the Bible, and going to church—staples evidently sufficient for his peers? That is, what did Wesley see that others did not; and perhaps more important, why did he long for it?

The point of his autobiographical narrative, however, was not to display the sharpest contrast possible between Wesley's life at Epworth and later at Charterhouse. The work of Luke Tyerman, a nineteenth-century biographer, is already well known—and criticized—for its claim that "Wesley entered Charterhouse a saint, and left it a sinner."[13] Wesley's own observations actually suggest much more continuity from one setting to the other, from rectory to school—especially in his religious practices and habits—than Tyerman was apparently willing to allow. The real issue seems to be, how could the later Wesley be dissatisfied with his life at Charterhouse, a life which was, for the most part, virtuous, disciplined, and quite comfortable? To put it another way, what more could there possibly be to religion that Wesley had not yet realized?

A keen interest in religious matters in general and in the supernatural in particular continued throughout Wesley's school days. Between December 1715 and January 1716, for example, while he was still at Charterhouse, he learned of a ghost that was supposedly haunting the rectory at Epworth. The inexplicable clatter of bottles breaking, the thump of footsteps on stairs, and the gobbling of turkeys at first frightened but then amused the Wesley children. The ghost, which was quite noisy during family prayers, was something of a Jacobite because it was most annoying when Samuel was praying for the king. Several family members reported that they had actually seen the ghost, whom Emilia dubbed "Old Jeffrey." To Susanna it resembled a headless badger, to Sukey and Hetty it appeared like a man in a long nightgown, and to Robin Brown it looked like a white rabbit. John's curiosity was so sparked by these reports from his mother and sisters, as well as from transcribing his father's diary, that he carefully examined all the evidence of this phenomenon and came to the conclusion that "Old Jeffrey" was indeed real and not simply the imaginings of his family or the malicious work of hateful neighbors.

With the stories of ghosts hardly forgotten, Charles Wesley made his way next year to the Westminster school in London, an academy at which his brother Samuel Jr. was an usher. Because of his taste for scholarship, Samuel Sr. eagerly sought whatever educational opportunities for his children that he could afford, and so he was naturally well pleased with the direction of Charles' education. Soon John would be ready for the university and his somewhat ambitious father hoped to ensure that he would gain entrance to no place less than Oxford University. With such a design in mind, Samuel arranged a meeting between his son and Dr. Sacheverell, who supposedly could provide a handsome recommendation. But from all reports the meeting between the well-connected scholar and the hopeful student did not go well. Sacheverell looked at the small stature of John Wesley and declared, "You are too young to go to the university, you cannot know Greek and Latin yet. Go back to school."[14] Wesley's response to such flippancy was immediate and frank: "I looked at him as David looked at Goliath, and despised him in my heart. I thought, 'If I do not know Greek and Latin better than you, I ought to go back to school indeed.'"[15]

Despite Dr. Sacheverell's gloomy assessment, John Wesley was admitted to Christ Church, Oxford University, in July 1720. As a gown-boy and graduate of Charterhouse, Wesley was entitled to forty pounds a year for three years and one hundred pounds for the fourth year.[16] But this sum was hardly sufficient for an Oxford student and so both Susanna and Samuel sent funds from time to time. Despite such support, John—perhaps taking after his father—was frequently in debt. Knowing that her son was occasionally troubled and dispirited at Christ Church due to his financial situation, Susanna offered words of both comfort and assurance: "Be not discouraged; do your duty, keep close to your studies, and hope for better days; perhaps notwithstanding all, we shall pick up a few crumbs for you before the end of the year."[17]

Lively and engaging, with a keen mind and a sharp wit, Wesley had several friends at Christ Church with whom he often took meals. His youthful manner was easy and light, marked by a taste both for conversation and for the diversions of the day. Like many other students, Wesley frequented the coffee house, rowed on the river, and played backgammon, billiards, chess, cards, and tennis. And on those rare occasions when both time and resources permitted, he would attend the theater. Mr. Badcock described the twenty-one-year-old Wesley in the following way: "[He was] the very sensible and acute collegian, baffling every man by the subtleties of [his] logic, and laughing at them for being so easily routed; a young fellow of the finest classical taste, of the most liberal and manly sentiments. [He was] gay and sprightly, with a turn for wit and humour."[18]

Here was a young man, in other words, who was obviously enjoying his youth, who was exploring an array of activities with a sense of wonder and ease. The seriousness and the meticulous use of time, so characteristic of the mature Wesley, would only come later. Indeed, it would take reading Jeremy Taylor's *Rules of Holy Living and Holy Dying* shortly after his residence at Christ Church, among other things, to precipitate such a change. And yet elements of that later seriousness, especially in religion, were present even during this period. Late one night, for instance, John Wesley had a lively conversation with the porter of Christ Church, which left a deep and lasting impression on him. For though the young Oxford student made a practice of attending public and private prayers, reading the Scriptures and other books of religion, as well as receiving Holy Communion at least three times a year as required by the university, he came to realize through this late-night dialogue "that there was something in religion which he had not found." That night, then, within the dimly lit halls of the college, John Wesley was intrigued, and his imagination was captivated. He was about to set out on a remarkable journey.

2

The Point of It All

The letters between John Wesley and his parents when he was about twenty-two years old reveal a growing seriousness on the part of John and the recognition, first by Susanna and then by Samuel, that their son was well suited for Anglican ordination. Interestingly enough, though Wesley in retrospect maintained that it was his father, Samuel, who pressed him to enter into holy orders, it was actually Susanna who raised the issue for the first time.[1] "I heartily wish you were in orders," she wrote in September 1724, "and could come and serve one of his [Samuel Sr.'s] churches. Then I should see you often, and could be more helpful to you than 'tis possible at a distance."[2]

Later, in February 1725, Susanna confessed to her son, "I think the sooner you are a deacon the better, because it may be an inducement to greater application in the study of practical divinity, which of all others I humbly conceive is the best study for candidates for orders."[3] Such counsel led Fitchett, an early twentieth-century biographer of Wesley, to conclude, "Here again is the same odd inversion of the true spiritual order. The ministerial office comes first, and fitness for it afterwards."[4] But in fairness to Susanna it must be noted that in the very same letter in which she linked deacon's orders to an inducement to practical divinity she also pointed out—and this is what Fitchett missed—that John should enter upon a serious examination of himself in order that he might know whether or not he had a reasonable hope of salvation in Jesus Christ. "This matter deserves great consideration in all," Susanna reasoned, "but especially those designed for the clergy [who] ought above all things to make their calling and election sure."[5]

When Samuel first learned of what John and Susanna had in mind, he was immediately opposed and sent his son this word of caution: "By all this you see I'm not for your going over hastily into orders. When I'm for your taking 'em, you shall know it."[6] In a touching letter which reveals something of her life with Samuel, Susanna confided to John in February 1725, "'Tis an unhappiness almost peculiar to our family, that your father and I seldom think alike. I approve the disposition of your mind, I think this season of Lent the most proper for your preparation for Orders."[7] Nevertheless, this unhappiness of which Susanna wrote was not to last long, for by the next month Samuel had already changed his mind—for whatever reason—and hoped that John would enter orders that summer. He also promised that he would gather up some money for his son's orders and "something more."[8]

During the time John Wesley was considering his call to the ministry of the Church of England, he encountered a "religious friend," one who helped him "to alter the whole form of [his] conversation, and to set in earnest upon a new life."[9] Just who was this religious friend who played such an important role in Wesley's life? One clue to this puzzle can perhaps be found in Wesley's habit of visiting the rectory at Stanton where he was friendly with Sally Kirkham, the rector's daughter. However, as Ward and Heitzenrater note, an equally strong case can be made for Robin Griffiths, the son of the Reverend John Griffiths of Broadway, Worcestershire, in the Cotswold Hills.[10] At any rate, this religious friend, whoever it was, helped Wesley to see the importance of inward holiness, the goal of religion, for which he now prayed.

Wesley's understanding of holiness in 1725 was also augmented by his reading of *The Imitation of Christ*, a spiritual classic attributed to Thomas à Kempis, a member of the Brethren of Common Life during the fifteenth century. This work, which was basically a manual to help the soul realize communion with God, both invited and repulsed Wesley. Indeed, Wesley's letters to his mother in May and June of 1725 show that he was concerned about the harshness of some of the teachings of *The Imitation of Christ*, in particular that we should supposedly be "perpetually miserable" in the world. Nevertheless, this classic had a profound influence on Wesley's life and thought:

> I met with Kempis's "Christian's Pattern." The nature and extent of inward religion, the religion of the heart, now appeared to me in a

stronger light than ever it had done before. I saw, that giving even all my life to God (supposing it possible to do this, and go no farther) would profit me nothing, unless I gave my heart, yea, all my heart, to him.

I saw, that "simplicity of intention, and purity of affection," one design in all we speak or do, and one desire ruling all our tempers, are indeed "the wings of the soul," without which she can never ascend to the mount of God.[11]

Here Wesley saw quite clearly the nature and extent of inward religion for the first time, that is, the importance of giving all his heart to God as well as the beauty of simplicity of intention. He was becoming much more spiritually sensitive and was now able to discern, in a way he had not done before, not only the subtle rhythms of the heart, but also the importance of the unseen, the eternal.

At about the same time Wesley was reading à Kempis, he became acquainted with the writings of Jeremy Taylor, especially with his *Rule and Exercise of Holy Living and Holy Dying* (1650–51). Born and raised in Cambridge, Jeremy Taylor was a conscientious cleric who eventually became chaplain to King Charles I. In time, Taylor was made an Anglican bishop (of Down, Connor, and Dromore), as well as vice-chancellor of Trinity College, Dublin. His *Rule and Exercise of Holy Living and Holy Dying*, like many of his other writings, breathed an air of simplicity, seriousness, and practicality that was indicative of much of seventeenth-century English spirituality. Ever concerned with the laity of the Church of England, Taylor, for the most part, targeted his efforts toward those who were not being served well by the local clergy.

In Taylor's writings, Wesley found once again, but in a slightly different way, what he had discovered in à Kempis, namely, the significance of purity of intention as well as the importance of thorough dedication to God. Accordingly, in reading several parts of *Holy Living and Holy Dying*, Wesley later reflected:

I was exceedingly affected; that part in particular which relates to purity of intention. Instantly I resolved to dedicate all my life to God, all my thoughts, and words, and actions; being thoroughly convinced, there was no medium; but that every part of my life (not some only) must either be a sacrifice to God, or myself, that is, in effect, to the devil.[12]

In this context, then, the Christian life is understood as devotion, as an entire dedication and consecration to the will of God. Here the Most High is the One toward whom the highest affections and tempers of the heart are directed.

Through encountering a religious friend and through reading à Kempis and Taylor, Wesley underwent what can best be described as a spiritual awakening. In 1725 Wesley understood, for the first time, that the end or goal of religion was *holiness*. He realized that religion entailed not simply outward exercise or duty, but also the tempers and affections of the heart, that it embraced not simply works of mercy, but works of piety as well, and that religion encompassed not merely external exercises but also inward devotion and dedication to God. All this and more Wesley learned as he prepared for ordination. It was truly a remarkable year.

When the elderly Wesley reflected back on his awakening in the pivotal year 1725, he couched it in the language of real Christianity. He explored his earlier religious experience along the lines of the distinction between being a nominal Christian and being a real one. For example, in his sermon "In What Sense We Are to Leave the World" (1784), Wesley stated:

> When it pleased God to give *me* a settled resolution to be not a *nominal* but a *real* Christian (being then about two and twenty years of age) my acquaintance were as ignorant of God as myself. But there was this difference: I knew my own ignorance; they did not know theirs. I faintly endeavoured to help them; but in vain. Meantime I found by sad experience that even their *harmless* conversation (so called) damped all my good resolutions. But how to get rid of them was the question, which I resolved in my mind again and again. I saw no possible way, unless it should please God to remove me to another college.[13]

This passage expresses the same judgments and sentiments as those of the young Wesley during 1725. The continuity here is not only striking, but it also reinforces the notion that on one level the early Wesley was dissatisfied not only with his own Christian experience, but with that of others as well. Some of Wesley's peers, both at Oxford and elsewhere, may have been content, even self-satisfied in their Christian walk, but clearly Wesley was not. Biographers who gloss over this early period, who discern an untroubled continuity from the Epworth rectory to Wesley's public ministry later, must ignore significant evidence to the contrary—and much of it from Wesley's own pen. Clearly, Wesley's discontent and yearning for the deeper things of God mark him as one who desired spiritual growth as a *movement* from one realization of grace to the next, who welcomed, in other words, what our own age has called a spiritual journey. In fact, Wesley's concern to go forward, to enjoy more deeply the grace of God, evident in early life as well as in his later years, is the stuff of which spiritual journeys are made.

This is not to suggest that Wesley's early Christian experience must be presented in an extremely negative fashion in order to highlight later developments, as Luke Tyerman once again did in his observation that "except for the first ten years of his childhood, he [Wesley] was up to the age of twenty-two . . . an habitual, if not profane and flagrant sinner."[14] On the contrary, growing up in a godly home, with pious parents as his tutors, Wesley was, with little doubt, as virtuous and moral as many of his peers. He was not a distinguished sinner, as some would have it. On the other hand, since Wesley had not comprehended the end or goal of religion, which is inward as well as outward holiness, until 1725, he obviously could not have learned this while at Epworth. To be sure, the mere fact that Wesley as a young man desired a deeper spiritual experience, to the point of expressing discontent over his current experience, demonstrates that his home life had prepared him well—why else would he have such desires?—but the point is, it had not provided all. Both aspects, then, need to be acknowledged and affirmed if we are to appreciate the subtle intricacies of Wesley's development.

It is one thing to understand the end or purpose of religion; it is quite another thing to realize this end in both thought and practice. And though Wesley by the time he was twenty-two understood the point of it all, that is, the goal of religion in the midst of its beliefs, doctrines, sacraments, works of piety and mercy, and the like, he didn't yet comprehend the proper means to realize the goal of holiness. In a letter to his mother on July 29, 1725, Wesley evidently has a limited and largely undeveloped view of the nature of faith:

> Faith is a species of belief, and belief is defined, an assent to a proposition upon rational grounds.... I call faith an assent upon rational grounds because I hold divine testimony to be the most reasonable of all evidence whatever. Faith must necessarily at length be resolved into reason.[15]

The next month, Susanna replied to her inquiring son, "All faith is an assent, but all assent is not faith. Some truths are self-evident, and we assent to them because they are so."[16] She then pointed out to John in November that faith is "an assent to the truth of whatever God hath been pleased to reveal, because he hath revealed it, and not because we understand it." John's response to these observations demonstrates that he was in basic agreement with Susanna on this issue. "I am, therefore, at length come over entirely to your opinion," he exclaims, "that saving faith (including practice) is an assent to what God has revealed because He had revealed it and not because the truth may be evinced by reason."[17]

Thus, during the year of his awakening, when he was becoming richly acquainted with the things of God, Wesley nevertheless—and oddly enough—held a limited, deficient view of faith. Granted assent is ever an aspect of vital, redeeming faith, but it can in no way be deemed the whole. That is, mere intellectual assent to the truths of the Christian faith, whether such truths be sustained by reason or by an appeal to the authority of Scripture, can never by itself be satisfactory, for it may leave the dispositions and affections of the heart virtually untouched. Assent, then, must ever be joined with trust, a trust which holds to God as the center of all value; *fides*, in other words, must be accompanied by *fiducia*. In addition, faith must be embraced as a spiritual sense, as a means to discern the things of God as depicted, for example, by the author of the book of Hebrews. However, several years after 1725 would pass before Wesley would comprehend all three elements of the nature of faith aright: as assent, as trust, and as a spiritual sense. In the meantime, he sought various ways and approaches, some of which he later rejected, to realize the holiness that had so captivated him.

With the blessings of Susanna and Samuel, John Wesley was finally ordained deacon of the Church of England on September 19, 1725. Bishop Potter, the son of a Yorkshire merchant, officiated. The newly ordained Wesley continued his studies at Oxford and was elected a Fellow of Lincoln College on March 17, 1726, to the great pleasure of his father: "What will be my fate before the summer is over, God knows; but wherever I am, my Jacky is Fellow of Lincoln."[18] Several months later, in November 1726, John was elected Greek lecturer and moderator of the classes. As a Greek lecturer, Wesley expounded selected passages of the New Testament to his undergraduate students. As a moderator, he presided over the daily "disputations" of Lincoln, which were forums for the critical examination of various topics. Studious and disciplined in many respects, Wesley received his master of arts degree on February 14, 1727, and he delivered three lectures: one on the souls of animals, a second on Julius Caesar, and a third on the love of God. Unfortunately, these early discourses have all been lost.

Oxford University, then as now, was something of a puzzle to outsiders. The heads of various colleges, for instance, were known by different names. At Christ Church, where Wesley first matriculated, the head was called the Dean. But at Lincoln College the head was known as the Rector. Being an Oxford "fellow," a don at Lincoln, Wesley naturally enjoyed some privileges such as opportunities for intellectual enhancement as well as a modest income. There were rules, of course, though not very many, the principal one being that the fellowship, with its title and stipend, had to be surrendered once one married.

In January 1727, while he was at Lincoln College and shortly before he received his master's degree, Wesley wrote to his mother looking to her, once again, for guidance in the area of practical divinity. Having drawn up a scheme of studies from which he did not intend to depart, Wesley related to Susanna that he had "perfectly come over to [her] opinion, that there are many truths it is not worth while to know."[19] Speculative studies, then, theological or otherwise, were quietly put aside. Earlier, in a letter to his older brother, Samuel Jr., Wesley had noted that "leisure and I have taken leave of one another: I propose to be busy as long as I live."[20] Accordingly, Wesley's energy and drive, always considerable, now had an even more focused direction.

But this January 1727 correspondence with his mother is valuable for another reason, for in it Wesley gives evidence, once again, of the seriousness with which he took the Christian faith, that he was in earnest to know, in an experiential and practical way, its deepest riches. Recounting an earlier conversation that he had with Robin Griffiths, Wesley observed:

> About a year and a half ago I stole out of company at eight in the evening with a young gentleman with whom I was intimate. As we took a turn in an aisle of St. Mary's Church, in expectation of a young lady's funeral with whom we were both acquainted, I asked him if he really thought himself my friend, and if he did, why he would not do me all the good he could. He began to protest, in which I cut him short by desiring him to oblige me in an instance which he could not deny to be in his own power—to let me have the pleasure of making him a whole Christian, to which I knew he was at least half persuaded already; that he could not do me a greater kindness, as both of us would be fully convinced when we came to follow that young woman.[21]

To be a "whole Christian," rather than half a one, was Wesley's desire for his closest friends, Robin Griffiths among them, and for himself as well. Such an emphasis made Wesley appear as earnest to his friends as he did eccentric to his enemies. How could a parson's son at Lincoln *not* be a whole Christian? The logic was inescapable for some, though it was doubted by Wesley himself.

In August 1727, Wesley left the comfortable environment of Oxford and headed for Lincolnshire to serve as his father's curate at Epworth and at Wroote. In this pastoral setting, Wesley saw little fruit to his ministry, but he continued to read spiritual and devotional literature. In 1729 (or perhaps in 1730) Wesley read William Law's *Christian Perfection* and *Serious Call to a Devout and Holy Life*. A godly man and something of a mystic, William Law was also a nonjuror—one who refused to take the required oaths of allegiance on the accession of George I, of the house of Hanover, to the throne of England. As a result, William Law lost his fellowship at Cambridge though he recovered somewhat by becoming the tutor of Edward Gibbon, the father of the famous historian.

Whereas the works of à Kempis and Taylor had shown Wesley the importance of purity of intention and of entire consecration to God, William Law's writings introduced him to the height, breadth, and depth of the law of God. Having a keen sense of the difference between the letter and the spirit, Wesley now understood the law of God not as a lifeless code, but as a life-giving gift that reflected the excellency of the divine being. Moreover, Wesley expressed in a by now familiar idiom the insights learned through reading the writings of William Law. Thus, several years later, in his *Plain Account of Christian Perfection* he pointed out,

> A year or two after, Mr. Law's "Christian Perfection" and "Serious Call" were put into my hands. These convinced me, more than ever, of the absolute impossibility of being half a Christian; and I determined, through his grace (the absolute necessity of which I was deeply sensible of) to be all-devoted to God, to give him all my soul, my body, and my substance.[22]

In another place, Wesley described his spiritual condition at this time and indicated, more specifically, what he took to be the relation between the law of God and redemption: "And by my continued endeavor to keep his whole law, inward and outward, to the utmost of my power, I was persuaded that I should be accepted of him, and that I was even then in a state of salvation."[23] But such notions of obedience to the law of God as the principal path to acceptance by God would not last.

Wesley went up to Oxford in July 1728 and was ordained priest in the Church of England on September 22 by Dr. Potter, the same bishop who had ordained him deacon earlier. Shortly after his ordination, Wesley returned to Epworth and Wroote to assist his father in pastoral duties. In the meantime, Charles Wesley was pursuing his studies at Christ Church, where he began to attend the weekly sacrament and to encourage a friend to do the same. A report from Charles in May 1729 of these pious activities encouraged Wesley to visit his brother and William Morgan. The members of this fledgling society not only attended the sacrament regularly, but they also prayed, studied together, and engaged in religious conversation. The seeds of what would later become Oxford Methodism were now being planted. Toward the end of the summer, however, the group dissipated as John and Charles went to Epworth and William Morgan to his home.

In a letter dated October 21, 1729, John Morley, the Rector of Lincoln, pointed out to Wesley that it was necessary for fellows to fulfill their duties at the college not in absentia but in person. The "interest of [the] college and obligation to statute,"[24] Morley counseled, required Wesley's return as well as the resumption of his duties—despite Samuel's need of a curate. In November 1729, after attending to his affairs, Wesley thus headed back for Oxford and, along with his brother Charles and William Morgan, continued where they had left off during the summer by meeting occasionally and by striving to keep the precepts of the university. The following spring Robert Kirkham joined their number and the group began to meet regularly. The little band was eventually referred to as "The Holy Club," "Godly Club," "Bible Moths," and "Supererogation Men." The term "Methodist" came later, about mid 1732, when John Bingham, of Christ Church, observed there is "a new set of Methodists sprung up amongst us."[25]

There is some dispute among historians as to what the name "Methodist" originally meant, for the evidence is ambiguous. When John reminisces about the movement in his sermon "On Laying the Foundation of the New Chapel," he associates the name with an ancient group of physicians who began to flourish at Rome during the time of Nero and who thought that "all diseases might be cured by a specific method of diet and exercise."[26] The name was also used, however, in the seventeenth century in a sermon at Lambeth in reference to a type of preaching evident in "plain packstaff Methodists, who despised all rhetoric."[27] To complicate matters further, Charles Wesley not only suggests a different dating for the initial use of the name Methodist, "This gained *me* the harmless name of Methodist. In half a year *after this* my brother left his curacy at Epworth and came to our assistance," but he also offers a different clue to its meaning, and contends that it was "bestowed upon himself and his friends because of their strict conformity to the method of study prescribed by the statutes of the University."[28]

Whatever the source of the term "Methodist," those called by this name eventually came to include—besides the Wesleys—John Clayton, George Whitefield, Benjamin Ingham, James Hervey, J. Broughton, John Whitelamb, John Gambold, Westley Hall, and Charles Kinchin, among others. From the very beginning this little religious society had focused on works of piety such as prayer, reading the Scriptures, and receiving the Lord's Supper as important means of grace, but with the addition of John Clayton to the group there was also an increasing emphasis on keeping the fasts (on Wednesdays and Fridays) of the ancient church. In regard to works of mercy, a constant concern as well, William Morgan augmented the Methodist practice by enjoining the Wesleys and others to visit the Oxford prisons, the Castle and the Bocardo for instance, as well as to work among the poor. Accordingly, as a part of their discipline and stewardship, the Oxford Methodists cut off all needless expense so that they could be of greater service to those in need. In fact, Wesley noted that it was the practice of the early Methodists to give away all that they had after they had provided for their own necessities. A clue perhaps to John Wesley's own behavior at the time can be found in his sermon "The More Excellent Way":

> One of [the Oxford Methodists] had thirty pounds a year. He lived on twenty-eight and gave away forty shillings. The next year receiving sixty pounds, he still lived on twenty-eight, and gave away two-and-thirty. The third year he received ninety pounds, and gave away sixty-two. The fourth year he received a hundred and twenty pounds. Still he lived as before on twenty-eight, and gave to the poor ninety-two. Was not this a more excellent way?[29]

Wesley's later reflections on the rise of Oxford Methodism are also significant because in them he underscores the importance he attached to being a scriptural Christian where the Bible constitutes the basic standard or norm of his life. In his *Plain Account of Christian Perfection*, for example, he states, "In the year 1729, I began not only to read, but to study, the Bible, as the one, the only standard of truth, and the only model of pure religion."[30] Elsewhere, in his sermon "On God's Vineyard," Wesley points out, "From the very beginning, from the time that four young men united together, each of them was *homo unius libri*—'A man of one book'.... They had one, and only one, rule of judgment.... They were one and all determined to be Bible-Christians."[31] Naturally, there were other ways of being a Christian in the eighteenth century, especially within the context of a large state church like the Church of England, but Wesley and the Oxford Methodists had chosen "the more narrow way." For their trouble they were mocked by their classmates, ridiculed on occasion, and called "Bible moths" and "Bible bigots."

Amid the gossip and the derision directed at the Methodists at Oxford was the charge that they lacked balance and perspective in the area of religion. "I have been charged with being too strict," Wesley confessed to Mrs. Pendarves in 1731, "with carrying things too far in religion, and laying burdens on myself, if not on others, which were neither necessary nor possible to be borne." Wesley dismissed such early criticism virtually out of hand and offered the reply "what is this but to change holiness itself into extravagance?"[32] But censure along these lines, that the discipline and rigor of the Methodists was indeed extreme, continued apace. Matters came to a head in 1732 with the death of William Morgan, one of the original Oxford Methodists, a death some claimed was due to excessive fasting. Obviously, Wesley could not dismiss such a charge so easily, and so in a carefully crafted letter, written to the deceased's father, Richard Sr. on October 18, 1732, Wesley attempted to clear up any lingering misunderstandings surrounding this untimely death and in the process offered an apologetic for Oxford Methodism.

But the allegations of rigor, exactitude, and scrupulosity continued. A few years later, in 1734, Richard Morgan, William's brother, complained to his father that the Methodists under Wesley's leadership "imagine they cannot be saved if they do not spend every hour, nay minute, of their lives in the service of God."[33] In an amusing coincidence in January of that same year, Wesley began what is called his "exacter" diary in which he conscientiously recorded "every hour in minute detail the resolutions broken and kept, his temper of devotion (on a rating scale from 1 to 9), his level of 'simplicity' and 'recollection,' in addition to the usual record of his reading, visiting, writing, conversing, and other activities."[34] Moreover, the rector of the College, Dr. Morley, cautioned Richard

Morgan Jr. against "Mr. Wesley's strict notions of religion," and told him that "the character of his Society prevented several from entering in the College."[35] In light of this counsel, Richard concluded in a letter to his father that if he continued under Wesley's tutoring, he would be ruined. In defense, Wesley wrote to Richard Morgan Sr. in 1734 and in the process articulated a well-developed, even beautiful, understanding of religion:

> I take religion to be, not the bare saying over so many prayers morning and evening, in public or in private; not anything superadded now and then to a careless or worldly life; but a constant ruling habit of soul; a renewal of our minds in the image of God; a recovery of the divine likeness; a still-increasing conformity of heart and life to the pattern of our most holy Redeemer.[36]

Here Wesley revealed the heart of it all, the throne room so to speak, that in the full round of activities of works of piety and of mercy, in the midst of rules and precepts, the Methodists were ever concerned with holiness, with the inculcation of holy love in both heart and life.

In a real sense, Wesley remained something of a paradox during this period both to himself and to others. For example, Mrs. Pendarves, the same woman to whom he wrote of the Methodists and their detractors, was also a part of a letter-writing circle in which Wesley himself participated during the early 1730s. A couple of other women took part in this group, namely, Sally Kirkham (Chapone) and Ann Granville. As with associations of this sort, there was some pretentiousness, to be sure, as members affected literary airs by using pseudonyms. John, for example, wrote as Cyrus; Charles, his brother, as Araspes; Sally Kirkham as Varanese; Ann Granville as Selima; and Mary Pendarves as Aspasia. In this setting, Wesley emerged not as a dour disciplinarian, caught up in rule and method, as his critics had viewed him, but as a deeply affectionate, kind, and sensitive soul. His letters could be touching, even poignant; his words empathetic, marked by deep compassion.

Wesley had known Sally Kirkham, one of his correspondents, from earlier days. In his early twenties, Wesley would often enjoy a picnic, a dance, or a game of cards at the Stanton rectory with

Sally and her siblings, Bob, Betty, and Damaris. From all accounts, Wesley's friendship with Sally was marked by tenderness, affection, and devotion, elements that continued—to the consternation of Susanna Wesley—even after Sally had married John Chapone, the local schoolmaster, in 1725. No doubt disappointed by this turn of events, Wesley sought reassurances from his friend, and so he met with Sally Chapone one evening and took the liberty to hold her hand while he laid his head gently on her breast. Moved with affection, Sally expressed her ongoing care for John: "If my husband should ever resent our freedom, which I am satisfied he never will; such an accident as this would make it necessary in some measure to restrain the appearance of the esteem I have to you, but the esteem as it is founded on reason and virtue and entirely agreeable to us both, no circumstance will ever make me alter."[37] Again, Sally professed that she loved Wesley "more than all mankind except her father and her husband." Betty, her sister, was likewise affected; and on one occasion when John asked if he could enjoy the same liberty with her as with his own sisters, she agreed and went off to bed that night with the words, "Good night, brother," on her lips.[38]

Touching as such scenes from Wesley's life are, it should be noted that he kept his early friendships with women, for the most part, on a spiritual level. Indeed, Sally Chapone, in considering the appropriateness of her ongoing relationship with Wesley, exclaimed, "I can't think it expedient, nor indeed lawful, to break off that acquaintance which is one of the strongest incentives I have to virtue."[39] Nevertheless, Susanna Wesley was not impressed with such professions of high-mindedness, and she feared that Sally—or her son—might soon desire things other than virtue. In fact, the correspondence between Wesley and this married woman outright alarmed Susanna: "The more I think of it, the less I approve it."[40]

While Wesley was participating in this letter-writing circle, he continued to look to Susanna for guidance in living the practical Christian life. Thinking of their earlier relationship as mother and child, and perhaps of a current problem with "inordinate affection" as well, he wrote to her in 1732, "If you could spare me only that little part of Thursday evening which you formerly bestowed on me in another manner, I doubt not but it would be as useful now for correcting my heart as it was then for forming my judgment." Remarkably, in this same letter, Wesley also hinted to his mother that perhaps all was not well in his relationships, for he related that the very thing he wanted to do was to "draw off my affections from this world, and fix them on a better."[41] Perhaps Susanna, who had been so helpful in the past, could ease her son's burden in the present as well.

As a kind and caring young man, Wesley was naturally well acquainted with the tempers and affections of the heart as is evidenced by his 1733 sermon "The Circumcision of the Heart." In this sermon, he describes holiness, the circumcision of the heart, as a "habitual disposition of the soul...which directly implies the being cleansed from sin, 'from all filthiness both of flesh and spirit,' and by consequence the being endued with those virtues which were also in Christ Jesus,"[42] especially faith, hope, love, and humility. Given his earlier letter to Susanna, perhaps Wesley's problem and fear was that the tempers and affections of his heart might be oriented—even overrun—by the love of the creature, in this instance by his devotion to several women, Sally Chapone among them, instead of being directed to God as their chief and proper end.

Moreover, Wesley's predicament was complicated precisely because he had not yet fully understood the proper way to be in a *relationship* with God through a trusting, humble, and gracious faith that is ever rooted in Christ, but he did indeed understand how to be in a relationship with a woman with all its stirrings of affection, flutterings of the heart, and sparking of desire. It is not surprising, then, that later when Wesley was in Georgia he would actually pit his love of the company of women against—or in competition with—his love of God; he would contrast, in particular, his devotion to Sophia Hopkey with his mission to serve God by proclaiming the gospel to the Indians. This was a pattern that Wesley not only continued throughout his life, but one that also caused him considerable difficulty. It emerged in the wake of his understanding of entire dedication to God not in an inclusive, embracing way, but in a nearly exclusive way, that God must not only be his highest love, but also, in a real sense, his only love.

Toward the end of 1734, Samuel Wesley Sr. became concerned about the ministry at Epworth and Wroote as well as about Susanna's financial condition, since he realized his health was failing. The elderly rector, therefore, made overtures to John to assume these pastoral duties—overtures that were flatly refused. In a letter to his father in November 1734, Wesley reasoned that "wherever I can be most holy myself, there, I am assured, I can most promote holiness in others. But I am equally assured there is no place under heaven so fit for my improvement as Oxford."[43] Samuel was stunned. He had hoped that his "legacy" in the parishes of Epworth and Wroote would continue. With a measure of frustration, Samuel replied to his reluctant son and complained that "it is not dear self, but the glory of God, and the different degrees of promoting it, which should be our main consideration and direction in the choice of any course of life."[44]

Failing here, the elderly Wesley wrote to Samuel Jr. and urged him to put some pressure on John. Like his father, Samuel Jr. accused his recalcitrant brother of self-love, of preoccupation with his own interests: "I see your love to yourself, but your love to your neighbour I do not see."[45] Beyond this, Samuel Jr. contended that Wesley had, in effect, obligated himself to undertake pastoral duties in his ordination vows. The irony—even the hypocrisy—of this argument was probably not lost on Wesley who knew that his brother had refused their father's earlier offer of pastoral duties, since their assumption would mean that he would have to resign as headmaster of Tiverton Grammar School, a position he greatly cherished. Nevertheless, Wesley took this argument offered by Samuel Jr. so seriously that he actually wrote to John Potter, Bishop of Oxford, to inquire whether this was so. "It doth not seem to me that at your ordination you engaged yourself to undertake the cure of any parish," the bishop replied, "provided you can as a clergyman better serve God and the Church in your present or some other station."[46] John forwarded this answer to his brother and triumphantly observed, "Now that I can, as a clergyman, better serve God and his Church in my present station, I have all reasonable evidence."[47]

But Samuel Sr. could not be so easily turned aside. John wrote again to his father in December 1734, offering more than twenty arguments as to why he should not assume the pastoral duties at Epworth and Wroote. Two points were integral to his position: first, Wesley not only repeats his claim that his own holiness (and therefore that of others) can best be promoted at Oxford, but he also offers a sophisticated, even profound, definition of holiness:

> By holiness I mean, not fasting, or bodily austerity, or any other external means of improvement, but that inward temper to which all these are subservient, a renewal of soul in the image of God. I mean a complex habit of lowliness, meekness, purity, faith, hope, and love of God and man. And I therefore believe that in the state wherein I am I can most promote this holiness in myself, because I now enjoy several advantages which are almost peculiar to it.[48]

As in his apologetic to Richard Morgan Sr., Wesley reveals to his father that his one end, his ultimate purpose, must ever be holiness and that which is most conducive to it.

Second, Wesley affirms that Oxford can further his spiritual growth by providing him with freedom from trifling acquaintances as well as the opportunity to be among real Christians. He elaborates:

> And this, I bless God, I can in some measure, so long as I avoid that bane of piety, the company of good sort of men, lukewarm Christians (as they are called), persons that have a great concern for, but no sense of, religion. But these insensibly undermine all my resolutions, and quite steal from me the little fervour I have; and I never come from among these "saints of the world"...faint, dissipated, and shorn of all my strength, but I say, "God deliver me from a half-Christian."[49]

This theme of being a real Christian, so evident during this period, would continue throughout Wesley's career with some important modifications along the way. Its continuity, as well as its modifications, provide insight into the character and purpose of this very complex and sophisticated man—a man who was governed by his heart as much as by his mind, by tempers and dispositions as much as by logic.

Unfortunately, Samuel Wesley Sr. died a little over four months after this final letter. In the interim, John reflected, hesitated, and then finally applied for the parishes. But it was too late. As he lay dying, Samuel spoke to John not of parishes or of legacies or even of the obedience required of a son. Instead, he whispered, "The inward witness, son, the inward witness; that is the proof, the strongest proof of Christianity."[50] But John understood him not.

3

The Education of a Virtuous and Affectionate Man

Shortly before Samuel Wesley died he asked his son John to present a copy of his *magnum opus*, an exposition on the book of Job, to Queen Caroline. In the fall of 1735, the queen received John Wesley with grace, thanked him for the gift, and noted that the book was "very prettily bound."[1] While Wesley was in London on this errand, he was solicited by the Reverend John Burton to become a missionary to the colony of Georgia. To this end, Burton also introduced Wesley to James Oglethorpe, Governor of the Georgia colony, who made a similar appeal.

After much thought, Wesley accepted the invitation to become a missionary and in a letter to Burton indicated two key reasons for doing so. First of all, Wesley maintained that his chief motive for going to Georgia, to which all the rest would be subordinate, was "the hope of saving my own soul. I hope to learn the true sense of the gospel of Christ by preaching it to the heathen."[2] By employing the phrase "the true sense of the gospel" in this context, Wesley reveals that there were vital dimensions of the good news of salvation that were for him, even at this time, unexplored. Second, the aspiring missionary declared that he could not expect to attain the same degree of holiness in England as he could in Georgia. Wesley had employed a similar argument earlier with respect to his father's offer of the Epworth living. Then Wesley had noted that he could be more holy at Oxford than in a parish at Epworth. Now he pointed out to Burton that he could be more holy in Georgia than in England—or, presumably, at Oxford. The places changed, but the logic remained the same.

On October 14, 1735, John Wesley, along with his brother Charles, recently ordained, headed out for Gravesend to depart for Georgia. Accompanying them were Benjamin Ingham of Queen's

College, Oxford, and Charles Delamotte, the son of a London merchant. At the Gravesend dock, the four boarded the *Simmonds* along with twenty-six Moravians and others. Though the *Simmonds* was no doubt a seaworthy vessel, Atlantic crossings in the eighteenth century could be quite dangerous. The sheer length of the voyage, for example, in this case from October 14 to February 5, allowed for the likelihood that the vessel would be pummeled by Atlantic storms that invariably arose during this season. On November 23, for instance, Wesley lay in his cabin only to be awakened by the tossing of the ship and the roaring of the wind, both of which showed him that he was, to use his own words, "unwilling to die."[3]

Though the voyage had been relatively smooth during December, the weather deteriorated in January 1736. Indeed, several powerful storms gathered in the Atlantic and buffeted the *Simmonds* during January 17 to 25. On the first day of this ordeal, Wesley recounted in his journal that "the sea broke over us from stem to stern, burst through the windows of the state cabin where three or four of us were, and covered us all over, though a bureau sheltered me from the main shock."[4] Nature, so powerful and awesome, once again evoked a response of fear from Wesley: "[I was] very uncertain whether I should wake alive, and much ashamed of my unwillingness to die." Yet another storm appeared during the evening of January 23, and Wesley confessed in his journal, "I could not but say to myself, 'How is it that thou hast no faith?' being still unwilling to die."[5] But the most powerful and frightening of all the storms en route to Georgia did not occur until two days later. The vivid details of Wesley's journal account, together with his several judgments, demonstrate that this storm in particular left an indelible impression on the anxious traveler. Wesley observed:

> In the midst of the psalm wherewith their service began the sea broke over, split the mainsail in pieces, covered the ship, and poured in between the decks, as if the great deep had already swallowed us up. A terrible screaming began among the English. The Germans calmly sung on. I asked one of them afterwards, "Was you not afraid?" He answered, "I thank God, no." I asked, "But were not your women and children afraid?" He replied mildly, "No; our women and children are not afraid to die."[6]

So taken was Wesley with the Moravian courage and serenity in the face of such great danger that he appended to this account, "This was the most glorious day which I have ever hitherto seen."[7]

Reflecting the next day, Wesley drew a connection between the powers of nature and the state of one's soul, between earthly tempests and spiritual distress. "I can conceive no difference comparable to that between a smooth and a rough sea," he writes, "except that which is between a mind calmed by the love of God and one torn up by the storms of earthly passions." In July 1736, when Wesley was in America he experienced a horrific thunder and lightning storm and confessed in his journal, once again, that he was "not fit to die."[8] A couple of weeks later, on a boat crossing the neck of St. Helena Sound off the coast of South Carolina, Wesley encountered yet another ominous storm. So furious was the wind and rain that it collapsed the mast of the ship, terrifying all on board. Of this incident, Wesley concluded with respect to himself, "How is it that thou hadst no faith?"[9]

This association between the forces of nature and spiritual condition—made repeatedly during this period—was extended by Wesley in linking fearlessness in the face of death with being a real Christian, not only in 1735 and 1736, but in his later years as well. In a letter to Miss Cummins on June 8, 1773, Wesley reasons as follows: "O make haste! Be a Christian, a real Bible Christian now! You may say, 'Nay, I am a Christian already.' I fear not. (See how freely I speak.) *A Christian is not afraid to die.* Are not you? Do you desire to depart and to be with Christ?"[10] Fearlessness in the face of death is a test that Wesley applied not only to his own religious experience, to and from Georgia, but one that he applied to others as well both early and late in his career. The continuity is striking.

As an Anglican priest, Wesley naturally practiced a number of spiritual disciplines, among them prayer, reading Scripture, and engaging in religious conversations. Other disciplines he employed involved some form of self-denial especially in the area of food and drink. For example, at the outset of the voyage, Wesley not only gave up drinking wine, but he also became a vegetarian, at least for a time, and subsisted chiefly on rice and biscuit. A couple of months into the voyage, Wesley carried his asceticism even further, no longer eating suppers, and found that this practice resulted in "no inconvenience."[11] Later he experimented to see if life could be sustained by only one sort of food. He and a few of his friends began to limit themselves to bread, with the result that they "were never more vigorous and healthy than while we tasted nothing else."[12] So convinced was Wesley about the value of asceticism and self-denial for Christian life and practice that one of the first actions he took when he arrived in Georgia was to help the crew (as required by the charter of Georgia) stave in the rum casks which had been aboard the *Simmonds*—an act that cost him the goodwill of some of the colonists.

Shortly after he arrived in Georgia in February 1736, Wesley sought advice regarding his moral and spiritual conduct from August Spangenberg, a Moravian pastor. Before he would answer, Spangenberg posed two questions to Wesley: first, "Have you the witness within yourself?" and second, "Does the Spirit of God bear witness with your spirit that you are a child of God?" Wesley was surprised by such probing questions and didn't know quite how to answer. Spangenberg nevertheless continued his queries, "Do you know Jesus Christ?" Wesley paused and said, "I know he is the Saviour of the world." "True," Spangenberg replied, "but do you know he has saved you?" Wesley's response was once again both weak and indecisive: "I hope he has died to save me." The kindly Moravian leader then brought matters to a head in a very pastoral way, asking, "Do you know yourself?" Wesley responded, "I do." But he later noted in his journal that he feared these were "vain words."[13]

This interview with Spangenberg, important in many respects, revealed to Wesley that he lacked the witness of the Holy Spirit that he was a child of God. Indeed, Wesley marveled at the assurance, the confidence, that Spangenberg seemed to have in matters of faith. This was the same sort of steady confidence that was displayed by the broader Moravian community on board the *Simmonds*. In the face of all this, Wesley was, of course, intrigued, and so he naturally wanted to learn more from these German-speaking people. To that end, Wesley was not only studying the German language—he had actually begun to do this at the very beginning of the voyage—but he also, along with Charles Delamotte, took up lodging with the Moravians in February 1736.

Such living arrangements gave Wesley ample opportunity to observe the day-to-day behavior of the Moravians since they were all in one room from morning until night. And he was remarkably impressed by what he saw, especially by the deep piety and humility of this godly people.

Though Wesley often spoke of his desire to preach to the Indians in America, his main duty, according to the wishes of the trustees of the colony, was to serve as a pastor to the colonists at Savannah. Ever energetic in the performance of his pastoral duties, Wesley began his ministry in Savannah on March 7, 1736, by preaching on the text of 1 Corinthians 13. In this new-world setting, Wesley's pastoral style included not only regular preaching, but also a meticulous adherence to the Anglican rubrics. He therefore gave notice of his design beforehand to celebrate the Lord's Supper every Sunday and holiday. Though the invitation to partake of the sacrament seemed to be for all who were heartily sorry for their sins, those who had not been episcopally baptized were simply refused admittance to the Lord's Table. The gracious and humble Johann Martin Bolzius, for example, pastor to the Salzburgers, was turned aside by Wesley not because he wasn't baptized, but because the sacrament had not been performed by a legitimate authority. Recalling this incident some twenty years later, Wesley remarked, "Can High Church bigotry go farther than this?"[14]

But there were other problems as well. Wesley not only baptized the children of dissenters while in Georgia (who had already been baptized in their own communions of faith), but he also insisted on triune immersion as the correct form of baptism. This last practice created conflict with Mrs. Parker, the wife of the Second Bailiff of Savannah, who refused to have her child dipped. Wesley, however, was as equally adamant on this point and so the child was eventually baptized by someone else. A couple of months later in June 1736, Mr. Horton took issue with Wesley's pastoral style and complained that his sermons were "satires on particular persons," and that the people "can't tell what religion you are of. They never heard of such a religion before."[15] Add to this Wesley's refusal to read the burial service over a dissenter and one can understand why many of the colonists were soon murmuring that their chaplain was really "a papist in disguise."[16]

Like his older brother, Charles Wesley encountered opposition to his ministry in Georgia, but it was of a very malicious kind. As secretary to the management committee of the colony and as the private secretary to Oglethorpe, Charles enjoyed the goodwill of the governor until Mrs. Hawkins and Mrs. Welch confessed to Charles that they both had had sexual relations with Oglethorpe. Then these women had the audacity to inform the governor that Charles was spreading this particular rumor among the people! Naturally, relations between Oglethorpe and Charles Wesley were strained until the governor had the good sense to ferret out the truth. Nevertheless, because of ill health, his inability to carry out his duties as secretary successfully, and the lingering effects of the gossip, Charles decided that it was best to return to England, and so he left Frederica, Georgia, in August 1736, having been in the colony only about six months.

Though John had not experienced the same level of misunderstanding, his own personality was remarkably complex. He could, therefore, easily be misunderstood—even by his close friends. On the one hand, he gave the appearance of being stern, perhaps even rigid, in the conduct of his pastoral duties. He seemed, for instance, to be self-assured with little doubt about the appropriateness of his ministerial style. And in one case in particular, concerning the death of an only child, Wesley could even appear outright cold and unthinking when he noted in his journal that this event was a "happy misfortune" for the father and that "the punishment was just."[17] On the other hand, Wesley was a deeply affectionate man—a trait which would have surprised not a few of his flock. While in Georgia, Wesley was introduced to Sophia Hopkey, the niece of Thomas Causton, the Chief Magistrate of Savannah. Almost from the start, Wesley and Miss Hopkey seemed to be romantically inclined toward each other. Thinking that a wife might do Wesley much good, Oglethorpe actually fostered the relationship between Wesley and this young woman—she was only eighteen at the time—by urging him to spend as much time with her as he could and by making sure that the two were placed in the same boat as they set out from Frederica to Savannah on October 25, 1736.

The boat ride set up by Oglethorpe, though relatively brief, precipitated a crisis for Wesley because he apparently already had tender feelings for Sophia. These feelings had arisen, no doubt, when she was his nurse during a brief illness in August 1736. Of this care, Wesley related that Miss Hopkey "sat by my bed, read several prayers, and prepared whatever I wanted with a diligence, care, and tenderness not to be expressed." So affected was he by the grace and charm of this woman, Wesley clearly saw the present danger to himself in the travel arrangements suggested by the governor. But he was reassured, first because the arrangements were not a matter of his own choice; second, he still had the same desire to live a single life; and third, he was persuaded that Sophia Hopkey intended to remain single.[18] In fact, the next morning as they crossed Doboy Sound, Wesley sought reassurance from Miss Hopkey that *her* intentions were noble and pure by posing to her the very same question, the very same standard, that he had so often applied to himself. "Miss Sophy," Wesley began, "are not you afraid to die?" "No, I don't desire to live any longer," she remarked almost without thinking: "O that God would let me go now! Then I should be at rest. In this world I expect nothing but misery."[19]

A few days after this voyage Wesley inquired of Sophia Hopkey to what extent she was engaged to a certain Mr. Mellichamp, who was from several reports a mean and violent man. "I have promised either to marry him or to marry no one at all," she declared. Wesley responded with both kindness and affection, with an expression more of a sudden wish, as he put it, than of any "forward design": "I should think myself happy if I was to spend my life with you." Miss Hopkey immediately burst into tears and whimpered, "I am every way unhappy. I won't have Tommy, for he is a bad man. And I can have none else."[20] She then cautioned Wesley not to speak any longer on this subject, for he did not realize the danger he was in, and the two ended their conversation with a psalm.

Since he was tutoring her in the areas of practical divinity and French, Wesley spent much time with Miss Hopkey. Such close and private contact allowed him to express both kindness and affection to this young woman. Sometimes, for instance, Wesley put his arm around her waist, at other times he took her by the hand, and on yet other occasions he even kissed her, which she seemed not to mind at all. The deepening intimacy of the relationship naturally encouraged Wesley, and he began to fear the prospect of inordinate affection. To put it another way, Wesley was concerned he might soon love the creature more than the Creator, or perhaps Miss Hopkey might deflect him from his high purpose and calling to preach the gospel among the Indians. So conflicted, torn by his devotion to this young woman and to the tasks of ministry as well, Wesley sought to manage his affections, the tempers of his heart, by means of rules and resolutions. In early November 1736, for example, he resolved never to touch Miss Hopkey any more. But just ten days later, Wesley took Sophia by the hand and "kissed her once or twice."[21]

To strengthen his resolve against undue affection, Wesley outlined several reasons for not marrying, which included that he did not think himself strong enough to live in the married state, he feared it would obstruct his design to be among the Indians, and he believed Miss Hopkey's own resolve not to marry "were it only on Mr. Mellichamp's account." Despite his resolutions and reasons, Wesley remained deeply troubled and divided on this matter, and so he turned to Mr. Toltschig, the pastor of the Moravians, in February 1737 and inquired whether he should break off so dangerous a relationship. The Moravian pastor asked Wesley what would be the result if he didn't break with Miss Hopkey. Wesley replied, "I fear I should marry her." To Wesley's astonishment Toltschig replied, "I don't see why you should not."[22] Was this encouragement? Was this the will of God expressed in the words of a reply? Should Wesley pursue the design of his heart? But Wesley's friends, Ingham and Delamotte, remained unconvinced. To be sure, they utterly rejected Toltschig's counsel. Wesley had sought comfort and peace from his friends, but in hearing divergent counsel, he was now as divided in heart and mind as ever.

Shortly after his meeting with Toltschig, Wesley met with Sophia Hopkey and related to her in a very honest way something of his distress. More specifically, he revealed that he couldn't take fire into his bosom and not be burned.[23] He, therefore, told her that he was going to retire for a while in order to seek the counsel of God. The next morning, February 8, Wesley headed for Savannah and "groaned under the weight of an unholy desire."[24] His heart was with Sophia all the while and he longed to see her. To strengthen his resolve, to restore a measure of serenity, Wesley once again reviewed his reasons for not marrying. But they were powerless to quiet a heart so disturbed, so moved by deep affection.

Back in his own garden less than a week later, Wesley confided to Sophia that he was determined not to marry until he had ministered to the Indians. This declaration of Wesley's intent apparently disturbed the young woman, for the next day she informed him in a rather cool manner that she would no longer accompany him at breakfast nor would she come to his house alone any more. And the following day, she declared that she no longer wished to study French. Despite these pronouncements, Miss Hopkey was still very emotionally tied to Wesley. When she learned about a week later that he was planning to return to England soon, she "changed color several times" and exclaimed, "What! Are you going to England? Then I have no tie to America left." When Wesley asked her about these words later, she responded in tears, "You are the best friend I ever had in the world."[25]

Though Miss Hopkey affirmed that she would no longer come to Wesley's house alone, she apparently thought it quite all right for Wesley to visit her *alone* at Mr. Causton's where she was staying. On one such occasion, on February 26, 1737, Wesley was so charmed by Sophia's "words, her eyes, her air, her every motion and gesture," that he feared if he had touched even her hand—which he didn't—"I know not what might have been the consequence." The next day, the affectionate minister was again alone with Miss Hopkey, and at the end of a very serious conversation, no doubt on spiritual matters, Wesley's resolutions completely failed. He took Sophia by the hand and kissed her twice. Shortly thereafter, Wesley's divided heart and will emerged yet again, destroying all sense of peace. He now concluded that he had acted foolishly; he was beset by scruples; he resolved once more by God's help to be "more wary in the future."[26]

By early March 1737 Wesley had begun to realize that his rules, resolutions, and reasons were powerless to tame or order the affections of his heart. Indeed, one sight, one thought of Sophia, one touch of her gentle hand and all his resolutions were quickly forgotten. Failing with internal controls, Wesley sought "external" ones to manage his relationship with Sophia. Accordingly, he turned to the lot, of which three were made: on one was written "Marry," on the second "Think not of it this year," and on the last (the one chosen) was written, "Think of it no more."[27] Another lot was drawn on a different question, which revealed that Wesley should visit Miss Hopkey only in the presence of Mr. Delamotte. Yet just three days later, Wesley saw Sophia walking between the door and the garden. "The evil Soul prevailed," as Wesley put it, and he spoke with her even though Delamotte was not present. The tête-à-tête was interrupted, however, by the entrance of Mrs. Causton—an interruption Wesley later described as enabling him to be "snatched as a brand out of fire."[28] The young missionary was more painfully aware than ever that his resolutions were unable to check the advances of his heart. Indeed, the next day in his journal he frankly confessed, "My resolutions remained. But how long? Yet a little longer, till another shock of temptation, and then I well knew they would break in sunder, as a thread of tow that has touched the fire."[29]

So matters stood until on March 9, 1737, Sophia informed Wesley, to his utter bewilderment, that she had given Mr. Williamson her consent to marry—"unless you have anything to object." Wesley soon thought to himself, "What if she mean, unless you will marry me? But I checked the thought with Miss Sophy is so sincere."[30] The stunned pastor returned home and paced in his garden; he sought peace but found none. "From the beginning of my life to this hour," Wesley confided to his journal, "I had not known one such as this." "God let loose my inordinate affection upon me," he painfully confessed, "and the poison thereof drank up my spirit.... To see her no more! That thought was as the piercings of a sword."[31] Nevertheless, to fulfill her expressed intention, and also in part to flee the Causton home, which she found unbearable, Sophia married Williamson, a man noted for neither grace nor piety, on March 12, 1737, in Purrysburg. Wesley's romantic life, at least for now, was clearly over.

If Wesley saw nothing but sincerity and grace in Sophia's character prior to her marriage, then afterward he seemed to find nothing but artfulness and dissimulation. Spurned by Sophia, or at the very least misguided by her, Wesley accused the newly wed Mrs.

Williamson of "insincerity before and ingratitude since her marriage."[32] Moreover, the probing and exacting pastor now discerned several ecclesiastical faults in Mrs. Williamson, the chief one being her several absences from the Lord's Supper. And on one occasion when she did receive the sacrament, on July 3, 1737, Wesley spoke with her immediately thereafter and informed her of several things he found reprovable in her behavior. That Wesley was actually building a case against Mrs. Williamson is evident by the remarks he made to her uncle, Mr. Causton: "Don't condemn me for doing in the execution of my office what I think it my duty to do.... What if I should ... repel one of your family from the Holy Communion?" The chief magistrate paid little heed to this warning and replied almost matter-of-factly, "If you repel me or my wife, I shall require a legal reason. But I shall not trouble myself about none else."[33]

Some of the things Wesley had found objectionable in Mrs. Williamson's behavior were her neglect of half the public service, of fasting, and of almost half the opportunities for receiving the Lord's Supper. Beyond this, Wesley disapproved of Sophia's lying and dissimulation especially with respect to Williamson, a man whom she had stated repeatedly that she had no design to marry. For these and other infractions, both ecclesiastical and moral, John Wesley publicly humiliated her by barring her from communion on August 7, 1737.

Though Thomas Causton had given assurances earlier to Wesley on this matter, he was, in fact, incensed. He therefore required that Wesley make known the reasons he had refused the Lord's Supper to his niece. This was something that Wesley was more than willing to do. He even wrote to Sophia to explain his procedure:

"So many as intend to be partakers of the Holy Communion shall signify their names to the Curate, at least some time the day before." This you did not do.

"And if any of these ... have done any wrong to his neighbours by word or deed, so that the congregation be thereby offended, the Curate ... shall advertise him that in any wise he presume not to come to the Lord's Table until he hath openly declared himself to have truly repented."[34]

Perhaps to protect the honor of his family, Causton floated the rumor that Wesley had denied his niece out of motives of revenge, having made several proposals of marriage to her that were all rejected in favor of those of Williamson. Soon a grand jury was gathered, composed of twenty-six persons, and ten indictments were posted against John Wesley in August 1737. Nothing, however, really came of this court action, and sensing that his ministry was effectively over, Wesley announced that he was returning to England, "there being no possibility as yet of instructing the Indians."[35] A half-hearted attempt was made to stop his departure until the courts were satisfied, but on December 2, 1737, Wesley, as he put it, "shook off the dust of my feet and left Georgia, after having preached the gospel (not as I ought, but as I was able) one year and nearly nine months."[36]

After a difficult land journey through South Carolina, Wesley boarded the *Samuel*, of which Captain Percy was the commander. On Christmas Eve the ship sailed over Charleston bar and soon lost sight of land. A few days later Wesley experienced what today might be referred to as an anxiety attack: "Finding the unaccountable apprehension of I know not what danger (the wind being small, and the sea smooth)...I cried earnestly for help and it pleased God as in a moment to restore peace to my soul." After this unsettling incident, Wesley observed that "whoever is uneasy on any account (bodily pain alone excepted) carries in himself his own conviction that he is so far an unbeliever." More particularly, Wesley added, "is he uneasy at the apprehension of death? Then he believeth not that 'to die is gain.'"[37]

En route to England in early January 1738, Wesley reviewed his entire ministry in Georgia, assessed his spiritual condition, and penned the following in his journal:

> By the most infallible of proofs, inward feeling, I am convinced:
> 1. Of unbelief, having no such faith in Christ as will prevent my heart from being troubled; which it could not be if I believed in God, and rightly believed also in him [i.e., Christ].
> 2. Of pride, throughout my life past, inasmuch as I thought I had what I find I have not.
> 3. Of gross irrecollection, inasmuch as in a storm I cry to God every moment, in a calm, not.

4. Of levity and luxuriancy of spirit, recurring whenever the pressure is taken off, and appearing by my speaking words not tending to edify; but most, by my manner of speaking of my enemies.[38]

Wesley then prayed for a faith that would entail serenity both in life and in death and for a humility that would fill his heart from that hour. "Give me faith or I die; give me a lowly spirit; otherwise *Mihi non sit suave vivere.*"[39]

Later, Wesley linked the issue of unbelief explicitly with the fear of death, a recurring theme during this period:

I went to America to convert the Indians; but Oh! who shall convert me? Who, what is he that will deliver me from this evil heart of unbelief? I have a fair summer religion. I can talk well; nay, and believe myself, while no danger is near: but let death look me in the face, and my spirit is troubled. Nor can I say, "To die is gain!"[40]

Moreover, Wesley associated the fear of death with painful doubt and fear as well as with the absence of peace due to sinning. He observed, "I fluctuated between obedience and disobedience: I had no heart, no vigour, no zeal in obeying; continually doubting whether I was right or wrong, and never out of perplexities and entanglements."[41] Wesley had hoped for spiritual power and victory. Instead, he was plagued by doubt and fear, and he often succumbed to the power of sin.

Though Wesley was an Anglican priest, though he was assiduous in his pastoral duties, and though he was in many respects a virtuous man while in Georgia, he yet comprehended in a very painful and honest way that he had not realized in his own life the extent of holiness which had so captured his imagination since 1725. Indeed, the disparity between the ideal of holiness and his actual practice repeatedly unsettled Wesley, was the cause of much anxiety and fear, and was perhaps fed by three important concerns during this period.

First of all, the ghosts of Wesley's rigid and insensitive pastoral style were perhaps coming back to haunt him. Should not an Anglican priest be more kind, loving, and tolerant in administering the means of grace? Again, how did Wesley's pastoral style in Georgia speak of holy love as the goal of all, and how did it evidence the fragrance of the gospel of Jesus Christ? Though it would take much time for Wesley to sort out these issues, it seems that en route to England he understood, at least on some level, the inappropriateness of some of his pastoral ministry.

Second, how could a man who had repeatedly expressed love and affection to his beloved, then turn around and humiliate both her and her family, not privately—which would have been bad enough—but publicly? Was this holy love? Was this the grace of the gospel? And did hiding behind the Anglican rubrics make this humiliation any more just or any less offensive? Wesley's conscience may have been unsettled on this account. He may have begun to doubt both his motives and actions in this whole affair, in a way that took away both his peace and assurance. Again, was this part of the root of Wesley's spiritual turmoil, his "anxiety attack," aboard the *Samuel?* Was a guilt that was not to be denied beginning to rear its ugly head? Questions such as these probably tormented Wesley on his homeward journey and immediately thereafter.

Third, as we have just seen, on board the *Samuel* Wesley now specifically connected the fear of death with disobedience and sinning. This means, of course, that all of the numerous references to the fear of death throughout the Georgia narrative cited here are indicative of Wesley's own spiritual state and in a very specific and remarkably telling way. That is, such references demonstrate quite clearly that Wesley was during all this time—despite all his good intentions and virtue—not someone who enjoyed the rich, sanctifying grace of God, that grace which makes one holy, but someone who was both an anxious and troubled sinner in the sight of a Holy God, a God whose "eyes are too pure to behold evil."

What makes the Georgia experience so fascinating, then, is that Wesley was obviously in earnest to live the Christian life in an exemplary way, to realize holiness even to the extent of the intentions of his heart, and yet he was repeatedly frustrated in this endeavor. As noted, Wesley had tried to manage his spiritual life as well as the tempers of his heart by reason, rule, and resolution, but in this he failed again and again. Like the person described by the apostle Paul in Romans 7:15 ("I do not understand my own actions. For I do not do what I want, but I do the very thing I hate"

[NRSV]), Wesley was of two minds and two wills while in Georgia. He lacked the simplicity, the purity of intention, which emerges from willing one thing preeminently; his loves, in other words, were disordered, divided, often at odds with each other. Few can doubt, after reading the Georgia narratives, that Wesley was dissatisfied at the time, neither happy nor content with his own life and character. And if holiness and happiness are intricately related—and they clearly are—then Wesley would simply have to find other means to actualize the holy love he had so earnestly sought. The Georgia experience had begun with great dreams; it ended with painful realities.

4

The Makings of a Saint

Chastened by his Georgia experience, unsettled by bouts of anxiety and fear, Wesley was in a pensive mood as the *Samuel* pulled into Deal Harbor in England on February 1, 1738. In his journal, he made four key observations, very somber in tone, about his spiritual state. Of the first, Wesley wrote, "It is now two years and almost four months since I left my native country in order to teach the Georgian Indians the nature of Christianity. But what have I learned myself in the meantime? Why (what I the least of all suspected), that I who went to America to convert others, was never myself converted to God."[1] Some earlier biographers have let such statements stand alone in order to underscore the gravity of Wesley's spiritual condition. Such a device is neither fair nor accurate. For much later, in 1774, Wesley appended a "disclaimer" to this journal account, which appeared right after the comment "I who went to America to convert others, was never myself converted to God." It read quite simply, "I am not sure of this." Accordingly, Wesley was neither sure that he wasn't converted to God while in Georgia, nor quite certain that he was. His doubt, in other words, left *both* possibilities open. And though Wesley would later insist that he rarely used the term "conversion," it actually surfaced several times in his writings, though admittedly more than half of these were quotations from other writers.

Wesley's second very humble and self-reflective observation on February 1 touched on his well-worked theme, even by this time, of what it means to be a (real) Christian. He wrote in his journal whether all his efforts

> make me acceptable to God? . . . Or that "I know nothing of myself," that I am, as touching outward, moral righteousness, blameless? Or (to come closer yet) the having a *rational conviction* of all the truths of Christianity? Does all this give me a claim to the holy, heavenly,

divine character of *a Christian?* By no means. If the oracles of God are true, if we are still to abide by "the law and the testimony," all these things, though when ennobled by faith in Christ they are holy, and just, and good, yet without it are "dung and dross."[2]

However, in 1774, Wesley added the disclaimer "I had even then the faith of a *servant,* though not that of a *son,*" to this autobiographical material. In other words, by the early 1740s—certainly not in early 1738—Wesley came to distinguish different grades or levels of faith. The retrospective in 1774, then, reveals that Wesley's spiritual condition at the beginning of 1738 was not as "dark" or as "despairing" as he had initially supposed. Wesley had, after all, a measure of both faith and grace. But was it *sanctifying* grace and faith that he had?

The third observation Wesley made in his journal at this time, the one most despairing and therefore the most inaccurate of all, simply stated, "I am 'a child of wrath,' an heir of hell."[3] Clearly, this language was much too strong, and it called for nuances of some sort. Not surprisingly, in 1774 Wesley attached the disclaimer, "I believe not," to this entry. Indeed, this young priest in early 1738 may not have realized the full extent of holiness that he had envisioned; he may have been continually buffeted by doubt and fear; but he was hardly a "child of wrath, an heir of hell." That much, at least, was clear.

And finally, as Wesley made these pointed observations in his journal, he indicated that the faith he wanted was "a sure trust and confidence in God, that through the merits of Christ my sins are forgiven, and I reconciled to the favour of God." The faith he wanted, he later noted in his disclaimer of 1774, was "the faith of a *son.*" In other words, Wesley wanted that faith, as he put it, "which none can have without knowing that he hath it. . . . For whosoever hath it is 'freed from sin.'"[4] So then, though Wesley at this time was clearly not a "child of wrath," neither was he a child of God. In fact, it was precisely the later Wesley, matured and steeped in age, who noted in retrospect that at the beginning of 1738, he desired nothing less than the "faith of a son," the faith of a child of God.

A couple of days later, after the passengers of the *Samuel* had debarked and Wesley was in London once more, he reflected that though the design for which he had set out to Georgia had not been realized—specifically his mission to the Indians—he trusted that God had "in some measure humbled me and proved me, and shown me what was in my heart."[5] Wesley, the Anglican cleric and sometime missionary, now not only had greater self-knowledge because of his experiences, but he was also very meek, perhaps even broken. The Georgia venture had clearly not been all negative—as some have supposed—for it prepared Wesley to be open, in a very humble and teachable way, to all that God had in store for him—and there was much in store.

On February 7, 1738, Wesley had the good fortune to meet Peter Böhler, a Moravian missionary, at the house of Mr. Weinantz, a Dutch merchant. Wesley later recorded the significance of this meeting in his journal with the comment, "A day much to be remembered."[6] Though this initial meeting was obviously important, Wesley did not understand all that Böhler had to relate on this occasion, and the Moravian even cautioned Wesley that his philosophy—whatever that meant—must "be purged away."[7] Apparently, Wesley was intrigued by Böhler's understanding of the *nature* of faith, and so he naturally wanted to learn more. In the meantime, however, Wesley continued in his old ways—those that had become habitual in Georgia—and he guided his spiritual life by rule and resolution (was this what Böhler had referred to as Wesley's "philosophy"?). Later that month, for example, Wesley wrote down and renewed his former resolutions, and he no doubt had the desire, if not the ability, to fulfill them all.

Next month Wesley encountered Peter Böhler again while visiting his brother Charles, who was sick at Oxford. On March 5, as a result of his conversation with the young Moravian, Wesley was clearly convinced of unbelief, "of the want of that faith whereby alone we are saved." Immediately it occurred to Wesley to leave off preaching, for how could he preach to others a faith that he, himself, lacked? Böhler reassured Wesley and counseled, "Preach faith *till* you have it, and then, *because* you have it you *will* preach faith."[8] Accordingly, the next day, March 6, Wesley began preaching this "new" doctrine though his heart was not fully in it. The first person to whom he offered salvation by faith *alone* was Mr. Clifford, a prisoner under the sentence of death.

Toward the end of the month, Peter Böhler explored the *nature* of saving faith in greater detail with Wesley by pointing out the two fruits which are inseparable from it, namely: holiness (freedom from the power of sin) and happiness (the peace and joy which emerge from a sense of forgiveness). Wesley searched his Greek Testament to see if this doctrine was of God, and by the end of April, when he met Böhler again, he had no objection to what the young Moravian said concerning the nature of saving faith, that it is "a sure trust and confidence which a man hath in God, that through the merits of Christ *his* sins are forgiven, and *he* reconciled to the favour of God."[9] But what Wesley still could not comprehend was how this faith could be instantaneous, given in a moment, as Böhler had suggested. Again, Wesley consulted the Bible and to his surprise he found "scarce any instances there of other than *instantaneous* conversions—scarce any other so slow as that of St. Paul." But it was not until after Wesley was faced with the evidence of several living witnesses that he forthrightly confessed, "Here ended my disputing. I could now only cry out, 'Lord, help thou my unbelief.'"[10] Southey, the great biographer of Wesley, was simply incredulous at this point. "Is it possible," he asked, "that a man of Wesley's acuteness should have studied the Scriptures as he had studied them, till the age of five-and-thirty, without perceiving that the conversions which they record are instantaneous?"[11]

At any rate, it is important to consider what Wesley meant by the instantaneous nature of saving faith, lest there be misunderstanding. Indeed, neither Böhler nor Wesley taught that believers must know the exact time of salvation, the precise day or hour of redemption. By way of analogy, one can fall in love with a person, know that one is truly in love, but be totally unaware when this love first began. But that one is indeed in love and that a *crucial* modification of the affections of the heart has taken place is not seriously doubted. Again, since we are finite creatures, existing in time and space, *any* actualization or realization of grace will have a moment within a larger frame of time, whether that moment is recognized or not. This, then, is perhaps part of the theological legacy that Böhler shared with Wesley. That is, grace must become actual, not simply possible; grace must be realized, not simply imagined; and the process—however long or difficult—must eventuate in the appropriation of the actual grace and favor of God.

In 1738, Peter Böhler founded a religious society at Fetter Lane in London. Wesley, himself, often preached in this setting and he listed eleven rules for the society, which included that members were to meet once a week, be divided into "bands" or little companies, and speak as "freely, plainly, and concisely" as they could concerning the real state of their hearts.[12] This society, like the Methodist societies established earlier at Oxford and in Georgia, underscored the basic truth that Christianity is a social religion, that "to turn it into a solitary one is to destroy it,"[13] and that the Christian faith ever prospers in accountable face-to-face fellowship.

Schooled in a Moravian-Lutheran understanding of faith, at least for a time, proclaiming a faith which by his own admission he yet lacked, and no longer confining himself to the Anglican forms of prayer, but now praying "indifferently" as he put it, John Wesley was something of a puzzle, an oddity, to both friends and foes alike. Mr. Broughton, for example, upon hearing Wesley explore the nature and fruits of saving faith, objected that "he could never think that [Wesley] had not faith, who had done and suffered such things."[14] Wesley encountered strong opposition in many Anglican pulpits, first at St. John the Evangelist and at St. Andrew's, Holborn, in February 1738 and then in May 1738 in numerous churches such as St. Katherine Cree, St. Lawrence's, St. Helen's, St. Ann's, St. John's Wapping, St. Benet's, St. Antholin's, and St. George's, Bloomsbury. All these churches said in effect to Wesley, "Preach here no more!" Ironically, though Wesley believed he finally had a suitable message to proclaim, he was now quickly losing his audience.

Wesley's relations, however, were strained not simply with various Anglican pastors but with William Law as well, a saintly man and something of a mystic, who had been his theological mentor up to this point. In a letter drafted on May 14, 1738, Wesley complained to Law that he had been preaching after the model of his two practical treatises (*A Practical Treatise upon Christian Perfection* and *A Serious Call to a Devout and Holy Life*) with little effect. Wesley granted that the law of God was holy, but no sooner did he try to fulfill it than he found "it was too high for man, and that by doing the works of this law no flesh living be justified." To remedy this situation, Wesley redoubled his efforts and used all the means of grace at his disposal, but still he was convinced that this was a law "whereby a man could not live, the law in our members continually warring against it, and bringing us into deeper captivity to the law of sin."[15]

Under this heavy yoke, Wesley confessed to William Law, he had continued until God directed him to a holy man (Peter Böhler) who proclaimed, "Believe, and thou shalt be saved. Believe in the Lord Jesus Christ with all thy heart and nothing shall be impossible to thee." Now Wesley clearly saw, at least on a cognitive if not on an affective level, that "faith, as well as the salvation it brings, is a free gift of God." Exasperated and perhaps even somewhat angry at this point, Wesley interrogated Law more pointedly, asking, "How [will you] answer it to our common Lord that you never gave me this advice?" "Why did I scarce ever hear you name the name of Christ?"[16] The heart of Wesley's criticism, however, concerned the *nature* of faith itself, and he accused William Law of not having enough spiritual sensitivity and insight to realize that under his tutelage Wesley did not even have saving faith:

> If you say you advised them because you knew I had faith already, verily, you knew nothing of me, you discerned not my spirit at all. I know that I had not faith. Unless the faith of a devil, the faith of a Judas, that speculative, notional, airy shadow which lives in the head, not the heart. But what is this to the living, justifying faith in the blood of Jesus? The faith that cleanseth from all sin, that gives us to have free access to the Father.[17]

Here Wesley, with earnestness and sincerity, distinguishes the faith which pertains to nominal Christianity, a "speculative, notional, airy shadow," under which he suffered for so long, from that which pertains, more properly, to a son or daughter of God, even "the living, justifying faith in the blood of Jesus." Granted elements of this language clearly call for more nuances as well as for a clearer articulation, especially when Wesley writes that justifying faith "cleanseth from *all* sin," but the basic idea that justifying faith, broadly speaking, entails happiness and holiness or power and peace was now clearly comprehended by Wesley. Why he had not understood all of this sooner was the substance of his complaint against William Law.

In the meantime, Charles Wesley, like his brother John, was well acquainted with Peter Böhler and had profited much from his spiritual care and direction. By early May 1738, for instance, Charles now understood the *nature* of that "one, true, living faith, whereby alone 'through grace we are saved.' "[18] Later that month as he began to read Luther's *Commentary on Galatians,* he confessed with some puzzlement in his journal, "Who would believe our Church had been founded on this important article of justification by faith alone? I am astonished I should ever think this a new doctrine; especially while our Articles and Homilies stand unrepealed, and the key of knowledge is not taken away." Again, like his older brother, Charles wanted not "an idle, dead faith, but a faith which works by love, and is necessarily productive of all good works and all holiness."[19]

On Friday, May 19, while Charles was ill in bed, a certain Mrs. Turner told him that he should not rise from his sickbed until he believed. Charles, wanting to know if the woman was sincere, questioned her faith: "Has God then bestowed faith upon you?" "Yes, he has," came the reply. Not yet satisfied, and in a way reminiscent of his older brother's probing questioning, Charles continued, "Then you are willing to die?" "I am, and would be glad to die in a moment," Mrs. Turner declared. This woman's testimony, this witness to the liberating graces of redemption, no doubt, prepared Charles in some measure for what was to come. Indeed, two days later, Charles heard someone come into his room while he lay in bed and say quite distinctly, "In the name of Jesus of Nazareth, arise, and believe, and thou shalt be healed of all thy infirmities."[20] Initially, Charles had thought it was Mrs. Musgrave, a friend, but it was actually Mrs. Turner, herself, who had spoken these words. Not knowing this, Charles asked Mrs. Turner to go downstairs and get Mrs. Musgrave. While she was gone, Charles had, as he put it, "a strange palpitation of heart," yet feared to say, "I believe, I believe!"[21] So significant was this actualization of the grace of God in the life of Charles Wesley that he subsequently referred to it in his journal as "the Day of Pentecost." Charles now understood the graciousness and power of the gospel not simply intellectually, but also in terms of his tempers and affections. His heart as well as his mind now belonged to the Savior.

Just a few days later, on May 24, 1738, John Wesley, like his brother Charles, also realized the fruits of redemptive grace. So significant was the realization of grace for Wesley at this time that he placed a "narrative insert" in his journal—a summary of his spiritual life before, as well as a detailed account of the events which took place after the meeting on Aldersgate Street on May 24, 1738. This literary device, as well as Wesley's specific reference to his Aldersgate experience over seven years later, in a letter to "John Smith" on December 30, 1745, indicate quite clearly the crucial nature of this event.[22]

In his spiritual summary, Wesley pointed out, among other things, that while he was at Savannah he was "beating the air," being ignorant of the righteousness which comes from Christ with the result that he sought to establish his own righteousness or justification "under the law."[23] "In this state," Wesley continues, "I was indeed fighting continually, but not conquering. Before, I had willingly served sin: now it was unwillingly, but still I served it." In this path marked by repeated spiritual defeat, by the continual dominance of sin, Wesley remained. In his own words, he "fell and rose and fell again." Wesley intuitively understood, however, that such a condition is not what scriptural Christianity has to offer, that the proper Christian faith, to use his own idiom, is marked by a victory and a peace he had not yet realized. Clearly, Wesley could have assured *himself* by remembering his ordination, or by noting his missionary experience as well as his other works of mercy, but he refused to do so—a refusal, by the way, which brought him much criticism. Instead, in deep humility and painful honesty, Wesley confessed to all, and to the surprise of many, that he was neither content with his own spiritual life nor was he willing to call it the proper Christian faith.

In light of these changes, some more telling than others, when Peter Böhler came along proclaiming a "new gospel," announcing deliverance to the captives, nothing less than freedom from the dominion of sin, Wesley eagerly embraced such a message. Remarkable as it seems, it was only then that he began to realize that there are two fruits inseparably connected with a living faith in Christ, namely, "dominion over sin, and constant peace from a sense of forgiveness."[24] Wesley wanted nothing less than a living faith in Christ which was "inseparable from a sense of pardon for all past, and freedom from all present sins." Twentieth-century biographers, for the most part, have focused simply on the former aspect, namely, assurance, and while this element is clearly present in the Aldersgate narrative, it is the latter element, freedom from the power of sin (in conjunction with assurance) which is actually the key to all that took place in Wesley's life at this time.

In his Aldersgate "narrative insert," Wesley relates that in the days just prior to May 24, 1738, his spirit was marked by "strange indifference, dullness, and coldness, and unusually frequent relapses into sin."[25] The contrast, which follows shortly, is striking. Just what happened on May 24, 1738, then, is best expressed by Wesley's own words:

> In the evening I went very unwillingly to a society in Aldersgate Street, where one was reading Luther's Preface to the Epistle to the Romans. About a quarter before nine, while he was describing the change which God works in the heart through faith in Christ, I felt my heart strangely warmed. I felt I did trust in Christ, Christ alone for salvation, and an assurance was given me that he had taken away *my* sins, even *mine,* and saved *me* from the law of sin and death.[26]

Observe once again that Wesley's own Aldersgate narrative does not simply highlight the element of assurance, but sees it in conjunction with the liberty of having been redeemed "from the law of sin and death." As a matter of fact, in the days which immediately followed his Aldersgate experience, Wesley—while not neglecting the importance of assurance—underscored the theme of spiritual victory in a way that he had not done before: "And herein I found the difference between this and my former state chiefly consisted," Wesley observed. "I was striving, yea fighting with all my might under the law, as well as under grace. But then I was sometimes, if not often, conquered; now, I was always conqueror." Again, on May 25, Wesley exclaimed, "But this I know, I have *now peace with God,* and *I sin not today.*" And on May 29, although feelings of joy were no longer evident, Wesley could yet profess, "I have *constant peace,* not one uneasy thought. And I have *freedom from sin,* not one unholy desire."[27]

On June 11, Wesley gave evidence of his new-found faith and delivered what can be called his "evangelical manifesto," as Albert Outler put it, before the venerable at St. Mary's, Oxford. His sermon, "Salvation by Faith," took Ephesians 2:8 as its text ("By grace are ye saved through faith") and considered three key questions. Of the first, "What faith it is through which we are saved?" Wesley underscored the truth that saving faith "is . . . not only an assent to the whole gospel of Christ, but also a full reliance on the blood of Christ, a trust in the merits of his life, death, and resurrection; a recumbency upon him as our atonement and our life, as *given for us*, and *living in us*."[28]

Of the second question, "What is the salvation which is through faith?" Wesley pointed out to his congregation at St. Mary's that the salvation of which Christianity speaks is a *present* salvation and that it entails nothing less than redemption from sin here and now: "Through faith that is in him (Christ) they are saved both from the guilt and from the power of it." Wesley elaborated:

> This then is the salvation which is through faith, even in the present world: a salvation from sin and the consequences of sin, both often expressed in the word "justification," which, taken in the largest sense, implies a deliverance from guilt and punishment, by the atonement of Christ actually applied to the soul of the sinner now believing on him, and a deliverance from the power of sin, through Christ "formed in his heart." So that he who is thus justified or saved by faith is indeed "born again."[29]

Much later Wesley expressed this vital truth of a *present* appropriation of grace, actualized in the warp and woof of life, even more forcefully in "A Blow at the Root: Or Christ Stabbed in the House of His Friends" (1762). In it, Wesley reasoned,

> No, it cannot be; none shall live with God, but he that now lives to God; none shall enjoy the glory of God in heaven, but he that bears the image of God on earth; none that is not saved from sin here can be saved from hell hereafter; none can see the kingdom of God above, unless the kingdom of God be in him below. Whosoever will reign with Christ in heaven, must have Christ reigning in him on earth.[30]

And of the third question, "How may we answer some objections?" Wesley considered many of the kinds of criticisms which might be in the minds of an eighteenth-century Anglican congregation, such as (1) this teaching will drive people to despair, and (2) it is an "uncomfortable doctrine." Of the first objection, Wesley related that it was, after all, beneficial if the doctrine of justification by faith drove people to despair of their own efforts, their own attempts at righteousness, so that they could then receive the justification which comes from God *alone*. And though Wesley replied to the second objection, from his imagined critics, by quoting a passage from the Anglican standards, the Thirty-nine Articles of Religion in particular ("that we are justified by faith only is a most wholesome doctrine and very full of comfort"), the influence of Moravianism and even of the Continental Reformation was evident throughout this sermon. In fact, so enthusiastic was Wesley at this time, in the first flush of his Aldersgate experience, that he even referred to Martin Luther as "that glorious champion of the Lord of Hosts," language that was eventually dropped from the 1746 edition of his sermons.

But all was not well. Though Wesley had profited much from his acquaintance with the Moravians, some of his theological and spiritual malaise *after* his Aldersgate experience was due, in large measure, to their erroneous teaching. For one thing, the Moravians had led Wesley to believe that justification, and the new birth which necessarily accompanies it, would eliminate not simply the power of sin, which was accurate, but the *being* of sin as well, which was not. Either that or Wesley had simply misunderstood them. For example, when Wesley described his spiritual condition en route to England on board the *Samuel*, he wrote with unreasonable expectation, "The faith I want is 'a sure trust and confidence in God, that through the merits of Christ my sins are forgiven, and I reconciled to the favour of God.' ... For whosoever hath it is 'freed from sin'; 'the *whole body of sin is destroyed*' in him."[31]

Moreover, in his sermon "The Almost Christian" (1741), Wesley portrayed the "altogether Christian" in a way that essentially confounded justification with entire sanctification. That is, Wesley portrayed the real Christian, ironically, in very unrealistic terms:

"'His delight is in the Lord' *his* Lord and his all," Wesley wrote, "to whom 'in everything he giveth thanks.' *All his* 'desire is unto God.'" And again, "Whosoever has this faith which 'purifies the heart,' by the power of God who dwelleth therein, from pride, anger, desire, 'from all unrighteousness,' 'from all filthiness of flesh and spirit' . . . is not *almost* only, but *together* a Christian."[32]

But these characteristics are apt descriptions not of the liberty of the new birth (which does indeed entail freedom from the power of sin) but of that of entire sanctification. Indeed, nowhere in Scripture is it affirmed that babes in Christ (not "fathers" or "mothers") would be free from the *presence* in their hearts of such unholy tempers as pride or anger. However, it would take Wesley considerable time to work out the proper distinctions: a justified person is freed from the *guilt* of sin, a regenerated one from its *power,* and the entirely sanctified from its *being.* So then, if freedom from all sin (even its *being*) as characterizing the real or altogether Christian was the substance of the gospel that Wesley preached from March to May 1738 and following, it is little wonder that he was told by various churches to "preach here no more."

Naive in some respects and not yet realizing the full legacy the Moravians had bequeathed to him, both the good and the bad, Wesley desired still greater contact with this people—especially after his Aldersgate experience. To this end, Wesley set out for Herrnhut, a Moravian settlement about thirty miles from Dresden, in the early summer of 1738. By July 4, Wesley had reached Marienborn where he conversed with Count Zinzendorf, the leader of the Moravians. A couple of days later he noted in his journal that he had encountered many living proofs of those who had been saved "from inward as well as outward sin."[33] Later in the month, as Wesley and his companions came to Weimar, the gatekeeper of the city asked why they were going so far as Herrnhut. No doubt to the puzzlement of the gatekeeper who looked at him quite hard, Wesley replied that they intended "to see the place where the Christians live." Finally, on August 1, 1738, Wesley and his friends came to the settlement of Herrnhut, which was on the border of what was then known as Bohemia.

At Herrnhut, Wesley became acquainted with the testimonies of Christian David, Michael Linner, and Arvid Gradin, among others.

Christian David, for instance, pointed out that though sin still stirred in him, though it still remained, it did not reign. This distinction was very helpful to Wesley, and he would later develop it with greater care and precision, but his expectations with respect to the fruits which normally flow from justification were still unreasonable at this time, for he expected that his heart would be virtually pure. Indeed, shortly after his trip to Herrnhut, in October 1738, Wesley wrote, "I dare not say I am a new creature in this respect. For other desires *arise* in my heart. But they do not reign."[34]

Michael Linner also complicated matters for Wesley by insisting that full assurance, which excludes all doubt and fear, accompanies justification by faith. Wesley had already been taught this misguided notion by the English Moravians. Moreover, the day before he preached the sermon "Salvation by Faith," at St. Mary's, he had received a letter which threw him into much perplexity. The letter maintained that whoever had *any* doubt or fear was not simply weak in faith, but "had no faith at all." Deeply troubled, Wesley comforted himself with the observation that the apostle Paul referred to some in the Corinthian church as "babes in Christ" even though they were in a sense "carnal." "Surely, then, these men had *some degree* of faith," Wesley insisted, "though it is plain their faith was but weak."[35] Nevertheless, Wesley remained troubled—and confused—for quite some time. When he was back in England during October 1738, Wesley was particularly and needlessly aggrieved because he lacked "the full assurance of faith."[36] Thus, the association of full assurance with justification by faith was the second cause of Wesley's discontent. This misguided notion, in conjunction with a confused doctrine of sin, help to explain, in part, Wesley's troubled spirit, his sadness and lack of joy, even after his Aldersgate experience.

By September 16, 1738, Wesley was back in England, and he was pleased to learn that the society at Fetter Lane had increased from ten to thirty-two members in his absence. However, during this same month, some of Wesley's naivete concerning the Moravians was beginning to wear off, for on September 27 or 28 he drafted a letter containing numerous criticisms in light of his recent visit. Among other things, Wesley noted the Moravian neglect of fasting, their levity in behavior, their failure to redeem the time, and their use of "cunning, guile, or dissimulation."[37] Nevertheless, because Wesley still had some doubt about the accuracy of these judgments, he quietly put this letter aside. Its substance, however, eventually became a part of a later and much more lengthy one (August 8, 1740)—which Wesley did send—and in which he criticized the Moravians for their numerous excesses.

During the latter part of October 1738 and following, Wesley also corresponded with his older brother Samuel Jr., who had objected to his understanding of salvation and what it means to be a Christian believer. For his part, John pointed out that he had some measure of the faith which brings "salvation, or victory over sin, and which implies peace and trust in God through Christ, but the witness of the Spirit I have not, but I patiently wait for it."[38] John also reaffirmed his definition of a Christian:

> By a Christian I mean one who so believes in Christ as that sin hath no more dominion over him. And in this obvious sense of the word I was not a Christian till May 24 last past. For till then sin had the dominion over me, although I fought with it continually; but since then, from that time to this, it hath not. Such is the free grace of God in Christ.[39]

Observe in this correspondence yet another specific reference to Wesley's Aldersgate experience of May 24, 1738, further evidence that something vital had occurred on that date. Also noteworthy is how Wesley underscores this event, this realization of grace, as the time when he became free from the power of sin, a deliverance which Wesley, himself, deemed one of the salient marks of the new birth. But Samuel Wesley Jr., like so many others, would have none of this. "Have you ever since continued sinless?" he asked. "Do you never, then, fall? Or do you mean no more than that you are free from presumptuous sins?" After these pointed questions, Samuel drew the only conclusion he could: "If the former, I deny it; if the latter, who disputes?"[40]

While this disagreement with his older brother was going on—and John, by the way, was not willing to give an inch—Wesley began more narrowly "to inquire what the doctrine of the Church of England is concerning the much controverted point of justification by faith."[41] After a careful reading and editing of the Anglican homilies, Wesley published an extract, suitable for use by a wide spectrum of readers, entitled *The Doctrine of Salvation, Faith, and Good Works Extracted from the Homilies of the Church of England*. A few months later he published Barnes' two treatises on justification by faith alone. The motivation and purpose behind the publication of these pieces on the theme of justification by faith can be understood in a number of ways.

First of all, if Wesley had initially imbibed a Moravian-Lutheran notion of justification by faith—which, by the way, he judged to be in accord with the teaching of his own church, though there are some subtle differences—then it must also be noted, for the sake of accuracy, that Wesley was also in earnest that such teaching be explicated, taught, and proclaimed by means of his own Anglican tradition.

Second, Wesley well knew that, like his brother Samuel, others would invariably take exception to the *fruits* which he maintained accompany justification and the new birth. In light of this, Wesley wanted to be able to give a reasoned defense of the liberty entailed in saving faith by appeal to the teachings of the Church of England itself. Naturally, in this endeavor, he became better acquainted not only with the doctrine of the Anglican Reformation in general, but also with the work and genius of Thomas Cranmer in particular, especially his *Homilies*.

Third, by November 1738, when Wesley published his extracts, he perhaps already had some sense that his understanding of assurance and other matters pertaining to the doctrine of salvation might need revision and that study would, therefore, be appropriate. For one thing, his ongoing coldness in the midst of prayer, his lack of joy, as well as his repeated doubts and fears, which he confessed to his friend Richard Viney at Oxford, reveal a problem either in Wesley's *experience* or in the *standards* he was applying to that experience—or perhaps in both. Moreover, Wesley's sadness, his heaviness, was compounded toward the end of the month when Charles Delamotte, one of his trusted friends who had accompanied him to Georgia, criticized him severely. Though Delamotte's judgments were much too harsh and negative, Wesley nevertheless wrote in his journal, "I was troubled."[42]

In late fall of 1738, Wesley hastened to London to greet George Whitefield, who was just returning from Georgia. Though Whitefield was Wesley's junior by about ten years, Wesley had grown close to this onetime Oxford servitor. Perhaps Wesley enjoyed Whitefield's ebullient spirit, his engaging style, and his easygoing manner. Like many others, Wesley was undoubtedly impressed with the preaching ability, the rhetorical powers and grace of Whitefield, who could sway the coldest congregation and move it to tears. Benjamin Franklin's advice to those who would hear this gifted preacher was to go with empty pockets lest they give all that they had. And it was reported by some that Whitefield could bring tears to a congregation's eyes just by pronouncing the word "Mesopotamia."

Creative and unconventional in many respects, George Whitefield had already undertaken the practice of field preaching in Bristol during March 1739. At first, Wesley was horrified at such a practice—with its grass, mud, and rain—and he noted that he "could scarce reconcile [himself] at first to this strange way of preaching." "I should have thought the saving of souls *almost a sin*," Wesley added, "if it had not been done *in a church*." Whitefield, however, was persuasive as usual. Though we don't know the substance of all that he said on this topic, Whitefield probably convinced Wesley that he could save more souls outside a church than within it, especially since Wesley was now being excluded from so many churches. At any rate, whatever Whitefield said worked. At four in the afternoon on April 2, 1739, Wesley, to use his own words, "submitted to 'be more vile' and proclaimed in the highways the glad tidings of salvation speaking from a little eminence in a ground adjoining to the city, to about three thousand people."[43] Just a few days earlier, Wesley had written to John Clayton and proclaimed that all the world was his parish: "I judge it meet, right, and my bounden duty to declare unto all that are willing to hear the glad tidings of salvation."[44] Now with the beginning of field preaching, his parish truly was boundless.

Some clues to the substance of what Wesley preached can be found in his journal of the period. In it, he writes on April 25 that he preached "to above two thousand at Baptist Mills" on the topic "Ye have not received the spirit of bondage again unto fear, but ye have received the Spirit of adoption, whereby we cry Abba, Father."[45] Thus, at the very outset of the Evangelical revival in Britain, Wesley preached freedom from the bondage or dominion of sin as part of the good news of the gospel. Whitefield, however, disagreed with Wesley on this issue—he held to more pessimistic notions—but their sharpest disagreement, theologically speaking, was yet to come.

Valuing their friendship, Wesley was undecided whether he should challenge the Calvinistic views of Whitefield so directly as to preach on the subject of free grace. To be sure, Whitefield would find the notion that salvation was available to all sinners very troubling. To break his indecision, Wesley cast lots on April 26, which indicated that he should "preach and print." Accordingly, a few days later, April 29, Wesley published the sermon "Free Grace" in Bristol. On the one hand, the sermon impugned Calvinist predestination and, on the other hand, affirmed that salvation is free for *all,* that all who are in *need* of Christ may come to the Savior. Naturally, George Whitefield was angered by this publication, and it caused a rift, not quickly healed, between the two principal leaders of the revival. No sooner had Wesley and Whitefield joined hands than they were already beginning to go their separate ways.

Despite the difficulties between Wesley and Whitefield, by April 1739, with the employment of field preaching, all the main ingredients for a revival in Britain were in place: preachers marked by holiness and love; a message of forgiveness, liberation, and peace; and willing listeners. Wesley, himself, had the first two ingredients by May 24, 1738; the last one not until April 2, 1739. However, all of these elements were necessary, none to the exclusion of the others, for promoting and sustaining the awakening that was soon to sweep across the land. Field preaching without Aldersgate, and its larger theological context, would have been empty, a proclamation of precept, rule and resolution, the confounding of sanctification with justification; Aldersgate without field preaching, on the other hand, would have been pointless, even self-indulgent. Reluctantly, Wesley had found his calling, and grace would make his calling sure.

5

Methodism Distinguished

That John Wesley, like George Whitefield, was a field preacher meant that he would not remain in one local church, but that he would itinerate throughout the British Isles. In the late spring of 1739, for instance, Wesley appeared in Bath, a town in the south of England near the Avon River. He had been cautioned by his friends not to preach there because he would probably be opposed by Beau Nash, the dandy of the city. Sure enough, Nash confronted Wesley, challenged his authority to preach, declared his meetings to be conventicles (illegal and seditious meetings), and claimed that Wesley's preaching frightened the people "out of their wits."[1]

Hardly disturbed at all, Wesley addressed each charge and then paid particular attention to the last. "Sir, did you ever hear me preach?" "No," Nash replied. "How then can you judge of what you never heard?" "Sir, by common report," Nash insisted. Wesley now turned the screws. "Give me leave, sir, to ask, Is not your name Nash?" "My name is Nash," the well-known gambler replied. "Sir, I dare not judge of you by common report," Wesley remarked. "I think it is not enough to judge by." Adding to this well-crafted rebuke, an old woman from the congregation exclaimed, "You, Mr. Nash, take care of your body. We take care of our souls, and for the food of our souls we come here."[2] Embarrassed and stymied, Nash replied not a word and walked away.

But perhaps there was something after all to Nash's claim that Wesley's preaching scared people "out of their wits." Just ten days after this encounter in Bath while Wesley was exhorting a society meeting in Wapping, some of the people collapsed, others trembled and quaked, and still others were "torn with a kind of convulsive motion in every part of their bodies, and that so violently that often four or five persons could not hold one of them." Of this occurrence, Wesley himself remarked, "I have seen many hysterical and many epileptic fits, but none of them were like these."[3] Naturally, reports of these disturbances spread throughout the land such that even Wesley's elder brother, Samuel Jr., began to ask, "Did these agitations ever begin during the use of any collects of the Church? Or during the preaching of any sermon that had before been preached within consecrated walls?" In a carefully written letter in October 1739, Wesley addressed his brother's several criticisms:

> How is it that you can't praise God for saving so many souls from death, and covering such a multitude of sins, unless he will begin this work within "consecrated walls"?...But I rejoice to find that God is everywhere. I love the rites and ceremonies of the Church. But I see, well-pleased, that our great Lord can work without them.[4]

For the sake of giving the gospel as wide a hearing as possible, Wesley not only, at times, put aside the "rites and ceremonies of the church," not only preached outside consecrated walls, but he also violated the parish boundaries of the Anglican Church to the annoyance and frustration of many of its clergy. Indeed, at one point Wesley had written to his brother Charles concerning his itinerancy: "God commands me to do good unto all men, to instruct the ignorant, reform the wicked, confirm the virtuous. Man commands me not to do this in another's parish; that is, in effect, not to do it at all."[5]

Wesley justified his "new measures," his innovative evangelistic techniques, to Charles and others by making a distinction between an ordinary call and an extraordinary one. "My ordinary call is my ordination by the bishop: 'Take thou authority to preach the Word of God.' My extraordinary call is witnessed by the works God doth by my ministry, which prove that he is with me of a truth in the exercise of my office."[6] To illustrate, a few years later, when Wesley, ironically, was barred from the pulpit at Epworth by John Romley, who had been the amanuensis to his father in compiling his commentary on Job, Wesley simply preached atop Samuel's tomb with wonderful and gracious effect: "I am well assured I did far more good to them by preaching three days on my father's tomb than I did by preaching three years in his pulpit."[7]

All during this period, then, Wesley believed he was in harmony with the Church of England. And when he was asked in September 1739 by a serious cleric in what points the Methodists differed from the Anglican Church, Wesley took this question not in terms of his "new measures" nor with respect to issues of church polity and governance, but simply in terms of doctrine: "The doctrines we preach are the doctrines of the Church of England," he replied, "indeed, the fundamental doctrines of the Church, clearly laid down, both in her Prayers, Articles, and Homilies."[8] The following month as Wesley preached on Acts 28:22 in Wales at Abergavenny, he related that he simply "described the plain old religion of the Church of England, which is now almost 'everywhere' spoken against, under the new name of 'Methodism.'"[9]

As the revival spread and as numerous Methodist societies were established as a result of Wesley's itinerancy, he was naturally at pains to provide suitable leadership. Initially, he had hoped that there would be sufficient Anglican clergy for the task, but even some of the former Oxford Methodists began to separate from Wesley in order to pursue distinct ministries. Faced with this predicament, Wesley asked John Cennick to go to Bristol and Kingswood in the summer of 1739 to assist in the work of the societies. Later, probably sometime in 1740, Thomas Maxfield began to preach in a society meeting during Wesley's absence—and without his permission. Upon his return, Wesley considered putting an end to this usurping practice, but his mother counseled otherwise: "Take care what you do with respect to that young man, for he is as surely called of God to preach, as you are."[10]

Because of Susanna's counsel and also because of the dire need of the societies themselves, Wesley eventually warmed to the idea of lay preaching, and so in September 1740 he began to employ the talents of Joseph Humphreys at the Foundery, a Methodist chapel. In solving one problem, however, Wesley quickly created another. For with the ministries of Cennick, Maxfield, Humphreys, and others, eighteenth-century Methodism was subjected to the same kind of criticism that had been leveled against Peter Waldo and the Poor Men of Lyons in the twelfth century. Not surprisingly, many of the Anglican clergy—for all sorts of reasons—resented such irregularity on the part of the Methodists, criticized the lack of education of many of Wesley's lay preachers, and therefore did not look kindly on the movement as a whole. Much later, in 1756, Wesley became so frustrated with the ongoing criticism against his preachers by Anglican clerics that he exclaimed, "Is not a lay preacher preferable to a drunken preacher, to a cursing, swearing preacher?"[11] The implication was clear to Wesley, if not to his detractors.

As the very structure of Methodism slowly evolved during 1739 and the early 1740s, so also the theology of Methodism under Wesley's leadership was being distinguished from various movements, Moravianism and Calvinism in particular. For example, in November 1739, Philipp Molther, who had been introduced to the Fetter Lane Society by James Hutton, began to teach society members, Jenny Chambers among them, that until they had justifying and regenerating faith, they should be "still" and leave off the means of grace such as attendance at the Lord's Supper. Mr. John Bray, a layperson and friend of the Wesleys, added his voice to Molther's teaching such that by the time John Wesley came back to London in December 1739 he found that "scarce one in ten retained his first love."[12]

Concerned about the effect of such preaching on the Fetter Lane Society, Wesley met with Molther in late December 1739. Two issues divided these men. First, Molther maintained that there are no degrees in faith and that no person has any degree of it before all things have become new. Wesley, on the other hand, maintained "that a man may have some degree of [faith] before all things in him are become new; before he has the full assurance of faith."[13] Second, Molther taught that the way to saving faith was to be "still," that is, not to use the means of grace such as attending church, receiving the Lord's Supper, fasting, praying, reading Scripture, and undertaking temporal and spiritual good. Wesley, on the other hand, affirmed the importance of all these means of grace as conducive to the reception of sanctifying grace, that grace which makes one *holy*.

In an attempt to heal the dissension at Fetter Lane, Wesley, along with his brother Charles, met with Molther on April 25, 1740. The Moravian leader, however, continued to insist that there are no degrees of faith, that no one has any faith "who has ever any doubt

or fear."[14] Moreover, Molther once again misprized, even deprecated, the means of grace. After this meeting, when Wesley saw the
ongoing results of these teachings on the life of the society—many
were indeed leaving off good works and neglecting the ordinances
of the church in order "to increase faith"—he took remedial action
by expounding the epistle of James. But it was to little avail.

Tensions within the Fetter Lane Society increased until on
July 16, 1740, Wesley was actually prohibited from preaching
there. "This place is taken for the Germans [Moravians]," it was
declared.[15] Frustrated with this turn of events, as well as with the
larger issues entailed, Wesley issued an ultimatum at Fetter Lane
four days later, at which point, along with eighteen or nineteen
others, mostly women, he left the society and began to meet at the
Foundery. In his ultimatum, Wesley not only criticized the "still-
ness" of the society, but he also impugned the notion that justifying faith excludes all doubt and fear. Wesley now understood that
justifying (as well as regenerating) faith does not imply the full
assurance of faith, as he, himself, had once mistakenly believed.
This teaching, part of the inheritance that Wesley had received
from the English Moravians, was decisively put aside.

As a result of the Fetter Lane incident, Wesley's relationship
with the Moravians was now marked by increasing ambiguity. On
the one hand, in a letter to Charles Wesley on April 21, 1741, John
listed several reasons for not joining the Moravians, including
their tendency toward *mystical* as opposed to scriptural religion,
their lack of self-denial, and their relative neglect of the means of
grace.[16] On the other hand, when Wesley had met with Peter
Böhler just a few weeks earlier, he was so impressed with the grace
and witness of this young man that he remarked, "I marvel how I
refrain from joining these men. I scarce ever see any of them but
my heart burns within me. I long to be with them. And yet I am
kept from them."[17]

Wesley's ties with the Moravians, however, soon became more
tenuous, as a result of his meeting with Count Zinzendorf at
Gray's Inn Walks on September 3. The Count, speaking in Latin,
maintained that the moment a believer is justified, "he is sanctified
wholly." Astonished, Wesley replied, "What! Does not every
believer, while he increases in love, increase equally in holi-

ness?...Is not therefore a father in Christ holier than a new-born babe?" The Count, who remained undisturbed, replied in words Wesley could not mistake: "Our whole justification, and sanctification, are in the same instant, and [the believer] receives neither more nor less."[18] Believers, in other words, are entirely sanctified when they are justified. The Christian life, then, is not characterized by *growth* in holiness.

By this point, Wesley well knew that other Moravians thought differently than Zinzendorf. When Wesley had met Peter Böhler and August Spangenberg earlier that May, they both insisted that the "old man," or carnal nature (original sin), is still present even in a child of God.[19] And though Wesley did not agree with Böhler and Spangenberg when they went on to maintain that the carnal nature necessarily remains until death, he did at least agree, certainly by the time of his conversation with Zinzendorf, that justified believers, those who are born of God, are not pure in heart, entirely sanctified. Wesley had finally put aside a notion to which he had once given assent, exclaiming on board the *Samuel,* "I want that faith which none can have without knowing that he hath it.... For whosoever hath it is 'freed from sin'; the *whole body of sin* is destroyed in him."[20] In short, Wesley had abandoned another Moravian doctrine, that Christian believers are freed from all sin, that they are entirely sanctified the moment they are justified. As a consequence of this and other matters, relations with Zinzendorf were strained, so much so that in 1745 the Count, in considering all the differences between the two communions of faith, declared that he and his people "had no connection with Mr. John and Charles Wesley."[21]

During the early days of the revival, Wesley distinguished the Methodism under his leadership and care not only from Moravianism but from Calvinism as well. As noted earlier, in April 1739 Wesley had published the sermon "Free Grace," to which his brother Charles appended a hymn on universal redemption. In these works, the Wesleys impugned the notions, so dear to Calvinists, of unconditional election, irresistible grace, and the final perseverance of the saints. Naturally, both pieces roiled Whitefield, who responded to them over a period of a year and a half. On September 25, 1740, for example, he wrote a letter that was eventually published under the title *The Perfectionist Examin'd.*[22] Copies of this letter were distributed to Wesley's congregation at the Foundery on February 1, 1741. After preaching that day, Wesley noted from the pulpit that the letter was a private one, published without Whitefield's permission, and so Wesley told the congregation that he would do just what Mr. Whitefield would do, tear up the letter. Wesley proceeded to do so, and the congregation followed suit.

Upon learning that Wesley and his congregation had torn up his letter, which championed Calvinist distinctives, Whitefield decided to publish a reply he had written earlier. *A Letter to the Rev. Mr. John Wesley in Answer to his Sermon entitled "Free Grace"* was originally written on December 24, 1740, but did not emerge publicly—Whitefield at the time had not wanted to aggravate an already difficult situation—until March 31, 1741, shortly after the letter-tearing episode at the Foundery. A few days earlier, Wesley had visited Whitefield in order to see for himself if the reports of his increasingly unkind behavior were true. Sure enough, Whitefield now seemed hardened in his opposition and told Wesley quite plainly that they preached "two different gospels" and that he, therefore, would not give Wesley "the right hand of fellowship." To make matters worse, Whitefield declared that he was resolved to preach against John and Charles Wesley whenever he preached at all.[23]

The division caused by the publication of the sermon "Free Grace" was eventually reflected in the organization of Lady Huntingdon's Connection, an association of Calvinist preachers, as well as to the founding of the Calvinistic Methodists in Wales. In fact, the controversy surrounding Whitefield and the Wesleys became so difficult and intense at points that even some of Wesley's early lay preachers, such as John Cennick and Joseph Humphreys, were persuaded to break ranks and to depart from their "father in the gospel."

Remarkably, when many biographers assess the Wesley-Whitefield relationship, they simply focus on the issues of free grace, election, and the like as if these represented the entirety of Whitefield's disagreement and censure. They do not. Indeed, a second cluster of issues highlights the important questions of just how a Christian is defined or understood in terms of sin and grace and whether or not those who are justified and born of God can expect to be cleansed from the being of sin, that is, perfected in love in this life.

Whitefield's position on these significant issues is actually difficult to assess because in corresponding with Wesley he continually shifted the question from "sinless perfection," that is, having a heart free from the *being* of sin, to the question of actually committing sin or being under its *power*. For example, Whitefield pointed out to Wesley in a letter drafted in September 1740 that "there must be Amalekites left in the Israelite's land to keep his soul in action,"[24] as if sin were necessary to keep one humble, as if a "heart bent towards backsliding," in opposition to and in rebellion against God, were necessary for holiness. Wesley, by the way, always deemed such reasoning to be specious. At any rate, Whitefield maintained that not only does the being of sin remain in the hearts of believers—thereby rejecting Wesley's notion of Christian perfection—but it also exercises sufficient dominion over believers such that they continually commit sin. Whitefield wrote to Wesley on one occasion, "I differ from your notion about not committing sin."[25] And in a letter on September 25, Whitefield made his meaning more clear: "If after conversion we can neither sin in thought, word, or deed, I do not know why our Lord taught us to pray to our heavenly Father, 'Forgive us our trespasses, etc.'"[26] Beyond this, in a letter to John dated March 17, 1741, Charles related how he, himself, had preached "on the believer's privilege, i.e. power over sin." Charles then invited Whitefield to the pulpit, at which point he proclaimed, once again, "the necessity of sinning."[27]

In light of these observations, some more telling than others, it is evident that John and Charles Wesley differed from George Whitefield not only about Christian perfection, but also about the liberty which pertains to a son or daughter of God. That is, not only was the whole matter of heart purity at stake, but also how a Christian believer is defined. With an eye to both of these issues, Wesley published his sermon "Christian Perfection" in 1741 and affirmed that "even babes in Christ are in such a sense perfect, or 'born of God'...as, first, not to commit sin."[28] A few years later,

Wesley also published "The Marks of the New Birth," in which he stated, "An immediate and constant fruit of this faith whereby we are born of God, a fruit which can in no wise be separated from it, no, not for an hour, is power over sin."[29] Whitefield, of course, disagreed with such notions and considered Wesley to be overoptimistic, even naive.

Both Wesley and Whitefield, however, tried to put the best face on a difficult situation, and in 1742 there was some measure of reconciliation. Both men continued to respect one another, and both never doubted the sincerity or the earnestness of the other. "I spent an agreeable hour with Mr. Whitefield," Wesley noted in his *Journal* in April 1742. "I believe he is sincere in all he says concerning his earnest desire of joining hand in hand with all that love Jesus Christ."[30] But the damage had been done. Wesley and Whitefield, though united in the necessity and importance of the revival, represented two very different theological traditions. They could work together, on occasion, and even consider each other friends, but there was always an element of unresolved tension.

Shortly after his struggles with the Moravians and Calvinists, while Wesley was expanding his ministry farther north into Newcastle, his mother became ill. Ever since the death of her husband, Susanna, being a poor widow, found it necessary to live with several of her children: first with Emilia, then with Samuel Jr., then with her daughter Martha and husband Westley Hall, and finally with John Wesley at the Foundery. As she lay on her deathbed at the Foundery on July 30, 1742, Susanna requested that those present—John Wesley among them—sing a psalm of praise to God "as soon as I am released."[31] After her death, an epitaph was inscribed on Susanna's original gravestone:

> True daughter of affliction she,
> Inured to pain and misery,
> Mourned a long night of griefs and fears
> A legal night of seventy years.
> The Father then revealed his Son,
> Him in the broken bread made known.
> She knew and felt her sins forgiven,
> And found the earnest of her heaven.[32]

The epitaph is surprising, even odd, for it reflects an implicit criticism of Susanna's spiritual life by her son Charles, who wrote these words, and her son John, who had the gravestone placed in Bunhill Fields. The epitaph, in effect, contends that Susanna was in the "legal state" for much of her life, until finally, around seventy years old, she received the *assurance* of faith that her sins were forgiven. For example, in the last stanza Charles apparently refers to the incident in which Susanna received the communion cup from her son-in-law Westley Hall in January 1740. As Hall was pronouncing the words "The blood of our Lord Jesus Christ which was given for thee," Susanna later noted that "these words struck through my heart, and I knew that God for Christ's sake had forgiven me all my sins."[33] However, had Susanna died in 1737, Charles probably would never have written such words nor would John have had such a stone placed. Perhaps the epitaph, then, tells us more about the spiritual experience of Charles and John Wesley, what they deemed to be the proper Christian faith, than it does of their mother's experience. Interestingly, Susanna's headstone was replaced in 1828 by the British Methodists, who substituted a less critical, more honorific epitaph.

During the mid 1740s, the ministry of John and Charles Wesley was beginning to bear considerable fruit. As Wesley put it, "The word of God ran as fire among the stubble; it was 'glorified' more and more; multitudes crying out, 'What must we do to be saved?'"[34] Indeed, the common folk of British society from London to Bristol to Newcastle were hungry for the message of the Wesleys. At first, in 1739, the Methodists were gathered into what was called the United Societies, a community which grew out of a request made to Wesley by several people as to how "to flee the wrath which is to come." Wesley described the purpose of the societies, which first emerged in London, as "a company of men 'having the form, and seeking the power of godliness.'"[35] The principal task of these meetings, then, as Henderson correctly points out, was one of instruction,[36] of communicating the vital truths of the Christian faith, especially to the poor and to those who had never seen the inside of an Anglican church.

In early 1742, Captain Foy suggested a solution to the payment of a debt on property that John Wesley held in Bristol, and out of his suggestion emerged what became known as the Methodist class meeting. As a subdivision of the larger Methodist society, the class meeting was often composed of up to twelve members. Leadership of the classes was open to women, and Elizabeth Ritchie, Hester Ann Rogers, Agnes Balmer, as well as Mary Bosanquet emerged as significant leaders.[37] The class meetings had something of a democratic flavor to them at least in the sense that class distinctions were ignored and one could, for example, move into a leadership role "on the basis of faithfulness alone."[38]

Unlike the more general society meeting, the purpose of the Methodist class was chiefly one of discipline, "to discern," as Wesley put it, "whether they [were] indeed working out their own salvation."[39] In 1743 Wesley published *The Nature and General Rules of the United Societies*, which indicated the normative value of the first two precepts of the natural law (avoid evil; do good) as well as the importance of the means of grace such as praying, reading the Bible, and receiving the Lord's Supper. These rules were offered not as the basis of justification, but as a guide, an illumination along the *way*, for those who were seeking the deeper graces of God. The class meeting, then, became one of the principal vehicles for determining whether or not the Methodists were walking according to the grace of God and the rules of the society. In 1743, for example, Wesley removed several persons from associating with the Methodists because it was learned (most probably in the class meetings) that they flouted the rules of the United Societies by habitual Sabbath-breaking, drunkenness, spouse abuse, habitual lying, speaking evil, and the like.[40] In this way, the Methodist vine, so to speak, was constantly pruned. So impressed was George Whitefield with this Methodist structure that in later life he attributed Wesley's greater success to it: "My Brother Wesley acted wisely," Whitefield exclaimed. "The souls that were awakened under his ministry he joined in class, and thus preserved the fruits of his labor. This I neglected, and my people are a rope of sand."[41]

In time the Methodist infrastructure came to include "bands" for those members who enjoyed the remission of their sins; "select societies," for those who walked in the light of God's countenance and were pressing toward Christian perfection; and "penitents," for those unfortunates who had fallen from grace yet desired renewal. In emphasizing both grace and discipline, the Methodist structure helped to prepare its members not only for the Kingdom of heaven, but also for service to the poor. By means of the society and class meetings, Wesley and the people called Methodists ministered to both the material and spiritual needs of the poor. Not only, for example, were the poor among the Methodists—for which they were smugly criticized by others—not only did Wesley establish a free medical dispensary for his people in 1746, the first of its kind in London, but he and the Methodists also proclaimed a gospel of liberation to the downtrodden: from the wrenching guilt of sin on the one hand, and from its crippling power on the other. Small wonder then that many of the poor of eighteenth-century Britain heard Wesley gladly.

But not all the poor were so well disposed to Wesley and the Methodists, nor were all so pleased with their efforts. As a new movement within the Church of England, Methodism was often and easily misunderstood by the sophisticated and unlettered alike. Wesley, for example, was accused of being a papist and in league with the Pretender, who was soon to attempt an invasion of England. Sadly, some of the clergy, perhaps out of a sense of jealousy or competition, played on such ignorance and even went so far as to hire rabble-rousers in places like Pensford and Oakhill. Mob action against the Methodists, not all of it clerically inspired, was both hateful and extensive. At Long Lane, for example, many of Wesley's congregation were thrust to and fro, and some were outright beaten; at Pensford in 1742, a bull was baited and sent into the crowd; that same year at "the Great Gardens," between Whitechapel and Coverlet's Fields, Wesley was met with a shower of stones, one of which struck him right between the eyes; at St. Ives in 1743, Wesley was struck yet again, this time with a blow on the right side of the head by the leader of a mob; at Costa Green in 1745 the swarm threw stones and dirt; and at Leeds, the rabble threw whatever was near at hand.

Having a keen sense of the providence of God, Wesley always looked a mob in the face. At both Wednesbury and Falmouth, for example, where the riots were quite severe, he soon had the chief instigators declaring their willingness to protect none other than

Wesley himself. At Wednesbury, the captain of the mob pro-claimed, "Sir, I will spend my life for you. Follow me, and not one soul here shall touch a hair of your head."[42] And at Falmouth, after the leader of the horde had heard Wesley explain himself, he swore that not a person should touch the preacher.[43]

News of riots precipitated by the mobs, along with reports of some of the earlier psychological responses to Wesley's preaching such as fainting, screaming, and wailing, spread throughout England, and several clergy, some in high office, became bitterly opposed to Methodism in general and to John Wesley in particu-lar. William Warburton, Bishop of Gloucester, complained that Wesley was an enthusiast, a fanatic, who was driving the common people mad. Moreover, Warburton thought that Wesley was espe-cially dangerous because "in parts and learning he is far superior to the rest."[44] For his part, Edmund Gibson, Bishop of London, claimed that the Methodists actually endangered the acceptance of religious truth by "making inward, secret, and sudden impulses the guides of their actions, resolutions, and designs."[45] Joseph Butler, Bishop of Bristol and Durham, and author of the famous *Analogy of Religion*, charged specifically that Wesley's doctrine of the Holy Spirit's witness to the believer—in other words Christian assurance—was yet another species of fanaticism. "The pretending to extraordinary revelations and gifts of the Holy Ghost is a horrid thing," Butler intoned, "a very horrid thing."[46]

Though Wesley was of the opinion "God made practical divin-ity necessary, the devil controversial,"[47] he knew quite well that he could not allow such criticism, coming from such high corners of the church, to go unanswered. To that end, Wesley wrote *An Earnest Appeal to Men of Reason and Religion* in 1743, *A Farther Appeal to Men of Reason and Religion* in 1744, and Parts II and III of the later work the following year. These writings, reminiscent of the work of the early church fathers, constitute an "apology," an attempt to offer a reasoned justification for the faith of the Methodists. Operating from the basic assumption that Methodism in large measure was a revitalization of primitive Christianity and a witness to the genius of the English Reformation, not only did Wesley proceed to demonstrate in his *Appeals* that Christianity is "founded on and in every way agreeable to eternal reason,"[48] but he also displayed the essential reasonableness of the love of God and neighbor, thereby uniting reason and vital piety.

The late Gerald Cragg, former Professor of Ecclesiastical History at Andover Newton Theological School, was surely correct in discerning the motif of real Christianity behind Wesley's energetic defense of Methodism in the *Appeals*. "Over against 'what is generally called Christianity,'" Cragg observed, "he [Wesley] set 'the true old Christianity, which, under the new name of Methodism, [was] everywhere spoken against.'"[49] To be sure, religious people in eighteenth-century England, clergy and laity alike, were "too often lulled into false security by the formal propriety of the faith they professed," with the result that they "knew little of true Christianity."[50] Wesley took such care in crafting the *Appeals*, then, precisely because he believed so much was at stake: not simply a defense of Methodism, not merely the reasonableness of the Christian faith, but also an apologetic for vital Christianity.

In 1744, the year of the first Methodist Conference—which considered what to teach, how to teach, and what to do—Wesley developed this motif of real Christianity yet further and actually went on the offensive in his sermon "Scriptural Christianity," preached at St. Mary's, Oxford, on August 24. No doubt frustrated by the repeated censure from his own church, Wesley was now poised to criticize the critics, to debunk the debunkers, in this very energetic, even caustic, sermon. To illustrate, Wesley moved unswervingly to his conclusion in this sermon by posing a number of increasingly pointed questions: "Where does this Christianity now exist? Where, I pray, do the Christians live?" "Is this city a Christian city? Is Christianity, *scriptural* Christianity, found here?" "Are you 'filled with the Holy Ghost'? With all those 'fruits of the Spirit' which your important office so indispensably requires?" "Do ye, brethren, abound in the fruits of the Spirit....Is this the general character of fellows of colleges?" "Once more: what shall we say concerning the youth of this place? Have you either the form or the power of Christian godliness?" On and on it went, to the bemusement of some who considered such barbs sport, and to the chagrin of others who considered them offensive.

After this series of probing questions, Wesley turned up the heat, and in a climax that was sure to roil the congregation, he referred to the youth of Oxford University as a "generation of *tri-flers;* triflers with God, with one another, and with your own souls."[51] The leaders of the university were naturally incensed. The vice-chancellor called for a copy of Wesley's sermon, and the bold preacher was henceforth removed from the rotation of fellows who were normally required to preach before the university. "I preached, I suppose the last time, at St. Mary's," Wesley wrote. "Be it so. I am now clear of the blood of these men. I have fully delivered my own soul."[52]

The content of the sermon "Scriptural Christianity," as well as the way in which it was delivered, clearly undermine the notion that John Wesley was a man who desired peace above all cost, that he was a Milquetoast cleric ever willing to gloss over the differences between the Methodists and others. Indeed, it was with boldness that Wesley had published the sermon "Free Grace" in 1739, to the dismay of the Calvinists. It was with determination in 1740 that Wesley had read a paper before the Fetter Lane Society and then walked out, to the consternation of the Moravians. And it was with remarkable honesty and courage that Wesley preached "Scriptural Christianity" at St. Mary's in 1744, to the censure of his own Anglican Church. Like his father, Samuel, and his mother, Susanna, John Wesley was a deeply principled person who was willing to suffer, to be criticized, rebuked, or even outright rejected for the sake of what he believed to be preeminently important, namely, the proper or real Christian faith, what he termed "scriptural Christianity."

Nevertheless, the boldness at St. Mary's in 1744 comes as something of a surprise simply because Wesley's correspondence and journal entries reveal that his theological views were actually changing, in flux, during this period, especially in the areas of justifying faith and assurance. How, then, could Wesley appear to be so confident, so self-assured, in his proclamations? In the area of justifying faith, a couple of years after "Scriptural Christianity" was preached, Wesley realized the need to develop a distinction between the faith of a servant and the faith of a child of God that would serve him well throughout his career. Thus, the Methodist Conference of 1746 not only described the faith of a servant, but it also linked such faith not with the love of God but with fear: "Who is a Jew, inwardly? A servant of God: One who sincerely obeys him out of fear. Whereas a Christian, inwardly, is a child of God: One who sincerely obeys him out of love."[53] The Conference then went on to declare that a person can be both sincere and penitent and still not be justified, indicating that the elements most often associated with the faith of a servant do not necessarily issue in justification.[54]

In short, though Wesley's understanding of the "faith of a servant" was still largely amorphous in the mid 1740s, he did explore the distinction between the spirit of bondage and the spirit of adoption, and this he was able to link, in later life, to a fuller understanding of "faith of a servant."[55] What then are the traits of the spirit of bondage displayed in the sermon "Spirit of Bondage and of Adoption" (1746), and which were later identified with the faith of a servant, in the sermon "Discoveries of Faith" (1788)? Those under a spirit of bondage, Wesley argues, feel sorrow and remorse; they fear death, the devil, and humanity; they desire to break free from the chains of sin, but cannot, and their cry of despair is typified by the Pauline expression, "O wretched man that I am! who shall deliver me from the body of this death?" In fact, in this sermon Wesley specifically identifies "this whole struggle of one who is 'under the law'" with the spirit of bondage and with the spiritual and psychological dynamics of Romans 7.[56] More to the point, these traits are hardly attributes that constitute real, scriptural Christianity, since, according to Wesley, a true Christian, at the very least, is one who believes in Christ such that "sin hath no more dominion over him."[57]

In the second area, Christian assurance, it should be clear by now that Wesley's views underwent significant modification from 1739 to 1747, precisely during the time he had preached so forcefully at Oxford. At least by December 1739, as noted, Wesley began to realize that there are both degrees of faith *and* degrees of assurance and that a child of God may exercise justifying faith mixed with both doubt and fear.[58] In other words, Wesley no longer associated justifying faith with full assurance. Indeed, less than a year after he began the practice of field preaching, he conceived the doctrine of justification by faith not in terms of full assurance but in terms of a *measure* of assurance.

However, in the mid 1740s, Wesley was still struggling with the question: Is this qualified assurance, occasionally marked by doubt and fear, necessary for redemption, for what he had called scriptural Christianity at St. Mary's? Here the picture becomes somewhat complicated. In a letter to John Bennet on June 1, 1744, Wesley stated, among other things, that none is a Christian who does not have the marks of a Christian, one of which is "the witness of God's Spirit with my spirit that I am a child of God."[59] Similarly, at the first Methodist conference that same year it was affirmed by those present that "all *true Christians* have such a faith as implies an assurance of God's love."[60] However, by the time of the next conference in 1745 the question was reconsidered and a slightly different answer was offered:

Q. 1. Is a sense of God's pardoning love absolutely necessary to our being in his favour? Or may there be some exempt cases?
A. We dare not say there are not.
Q. 2. Is it necessary to inward and outward holiness?
A. We incline to think it is.[61]

In a similar vein, the conference Minutes of 1747 noted that there may be exempt cases, that justifying faith may not always be accompanied by a measure of assurance. But the conference then offered this caution: "It is dangerous to ground a general doctrine on a *few* particular experiments."[62] In addition, although this conference, like the one in 1745, recognized that there are exceptional cases, it clarified its meaning and affirmed, "But this we know, if Christ is not revealed in them [by the Holy Spirit], they are not yet Christian believers."[63] In 1745, though this was a year of many changes, Wesley still had not retreated from his teaching that assurance is a vital ingredient of the *true* Christian faith, as evidenced by his remarks in a letter to "John Smith": "No man can be a *true* Christian without such an inspiration of the Holy Ghost as fills his heart with peace and joy and love, which he who perceives not has it not. This is the point for which alone I contend; and this I take to be the very foundation of Christianity."[64] Moreover, in 1747, Wesley continued this emphasis, once again in a letter to "John Smith": "The sum of what I offered before concerning perceptible inspiration was this: '*Every* Christian believer has a perceptible testimony of God's Spirit that he is a child of God.'"[65]

In light of the preceding, it is clear that Wesley even after 1745 still identified, for the most part, the assurance that one's sins are forgiven as integral to the proper Christian faith. Not surprising, then, in a revealing letter to his brother Charles, written a month after the 1747 conference, John illustrated his doctrine of assurance by pointing out "(1) that there is such an explicit assurance; (2) that it is the common privilege of *real Christians;* (3) that it is *the proper Christian faith,* which purifieth the heart and overcometh the world."[66] In other words, the observation that there are exceptions to Wesley's normal association of justification by faith and a measure of assurance is accurate; however, that he identified this faith which lacks the witness of the Spirit with real, proper Christianity is not.

So then, all that Wesley had proclaimed in his last university sermon, "Scriptural Christianity" ("Do we know Jesus Christ? Hath God 'revealed his Son in us'?"),[67] was accurate so long as the focus was on *scriptural* Christianity, the very title of the sermon. In other words, even though Wesley's views were in flux during this period, some important elements of his doctrine of salvation remained constant. Wesley's boldness, then, in proclaiming "*scriptural* Christianity" at Oxford was, in fact, warranted.

6

Settling Down

In traveling throughout Britain as an itinerant evangelist, in setting up class meetings in distant parts of the land, Wesley had the opportunity to be among the nation's poor. Knowing the downtrodden and their plight firsthand instead of simply by hearsay, Wesley observed, "So wickedly, devilishly false is that common objection, 'They are poor only because they are idle.'"[1] In fact, Wesley often associated many of the highest graces of the Christian faith such as humility, kindness, and patience with the poor, while, on the other hand, he criticized the rich for their *idleness*, pride, and self-satisfaction. Judging from a careful reading of his journals and letters, one gets the sense that Wesley was actually uncomfortable among the rich. "There is so much paint and affectation, so many unmeaning words and senseless customs among people of rank,"[2] he observed. And yet Wesley loved to be among the poor, perhaps because he found them most open of all to the glad tidings of salvation.

Though John Wesley genuinely loved the downtrodden and dedicated his gifts and energies to their service, this class of people in eighteenth-century Britain could at times be manipulated by the "middling classes" and by the rich for disreputable ends. At other times, the common people would add their own voices and numbers to the rabble-rousers of the day, simply out of ignorance or out of a sense of boredom and futility due to their awful lot in life. Accordingly, opposition to Wesley's preaching and evangelistic activity remained considerable and mob actions, so noisome in many ways, continued apace. Shepton Mallet, Roughlee, Bolton, Newlyn, and Hammond's Marsh all erupted in paroxysms of hatred during the latter part of the 1740s and the early part of the 1750s.

Help for Wesley's cause, the right to proclaim the gospel undisturbed by lawlessness and chaos, came indirectly from action taken by no one less than King George II, who declared that "no man in his dominions should be persecuted on account of religion while he sat on the throne." Once this declaration was made known, and due to the vigorous action of the Middlesex magistrates, "the persecution of the Methodists by mobs in process of time ceased in London."[3] Indeed, using what resources he had in confronting the mob, Wesley often appealed to the law of the land, the good order of the realm—as, for example, when he was in Ireland in 1750. Experiencing much difficulty in the city of Cork in particular, and sensing the possibility that his design of preaching the gospel might be thwarted, Wesley wrote to the Mayor of Cork, "I fear God and honour the King. I earnestly desire to be at peace with all men. I have not willingly given any offence, either to the magistrates, the clergy, or any of the inhabitants of the city of Cork."[4] And in 1752, while Wesley was in Chester, England, after he had learned that the mob had pulled down the house in which he had preached earlier, he simply inquired, "Were there no magistrates in the city?"[5]

In the face of the many trials and frustrations of an evangelist, Wesley took comfort from several friendships with evangelical Anglican clergy who remained willing to be associated with the Methodists—such people as Vincent Perronet (Shoreham), Samuel Walker (Truro), and William Grimshaw (Haworth), among others.[6] Such friendships were naturally very important to Wesley, for they provided him with opportunities for advice, support, and even correction. Therefore, the picture of a heroic Wesley who struggled alone, who was dependent largely on his own resources and designs, is a myth that bears little relation to the historical record. John Wesley's evangelistic activity, in the midst of the eighteenth-century revival with all its many obstacles and difficulties, was sustained by a network of nurturing, supportive relationships. Wesley not only sought the counsel of Vincent Perronet, for example, but he also took pride in enumerating to him the rules and discipline of Kingswood, the school Wesley had established in 1748 near Bristol for the sons of colliers.

In time Perronet came to be one of Wesley's most trusted friends, and both John and his brother Charles were welcomed in the pulpit of the small church at Shoreham in Kent. Interested in the theology and discipline of the Methodists, Vincent Perronet attended the Annual Conference in 1747, and Wesley was so impressed with this regard that he addressed his *Plain Account of the People Called Methodists* (1749), to the vicar of Shoreham. In this piece, Wesley revealed to Perronet, as well as to a much broader audience, that his chief design—like that of his brother Charles— in embarking on a preaching career in London and elsewhere more than ten years before was, as he put it, to "convince those who would hear what *true* Christianity was, and to *persuade* them to embrace it."[7] And to the charge that Wesley was dividing the Church of England by "gathering churches out of churches," through the establishment of Methodist societies, Wesley responded by rejecting the very premise that the Anglican Church was simply composed of sincere and devout Christians:

> If you mean only "gathering people out of buildings called churches," it is. But if you mean dividing Christians from Christians, and so destroying Christian fellowship, it is not. For, (1) these were not Christians before they were thus joined. Most of them were barefaced heathens. (2) Neither are they Christians from whom you suppose them to be divided. You will not look at me in the face and say they are. What! Drunken Christians? Cursing and swearing Christians? Lying Christians? Cheating Christians? If these are Christians at all, they are *devil Christians*.[8]

A few years later Wesley wrote to his friend Ebenezer Blackwell, a London businessman, on the same theme and noted the gentle-man's strong desire "to be not almost but altogether a Christian."[9] In fact, the more intimate Wesley was with his friends, the more willing was he to discuss the important matter of the state of their souls and often in a very open and forthright manner.

As a man who was sensitive, kind, and deeply aware of the tempers and affections of the heart, Wesley naturally had important relationships with women. Wesley was attracted to the opposite sex and was perhaps even oriented toward the female psyche in a way that few men of his times could understand. However, precisely because Wesley understood the language of the heart so well, he at times judged his relationship with women to be competing with, even able to displace, the love of God. When such fears arose, Wesley would often wax eloquent on the dangers of inordinate affection, the specter of loving the creature more than the Creator. For Wesley, all human love had to be properly ordered, directed to its highest end, namely, the love of God. Remarkably, this principle made Wesley look hesitant, unsure of himself, and perhaps even insincere at times to some of his female companions. Recall, for example, while he was in Georgia, Wesley as a reluctant suitor basically pitted his dedication to God and the tasks of ministry against his desire for a possible marriage with Sophia Hopkey ("I am resolved, Miss Sophy, if I marry at all, not to do it till I have been among the Indians").[10] And much later, in 1748, Wesley displayed remarkable continuity by maintaining that marriage *necessitated* a loss in the soul, a notion that did not set well with his lay preachers, many of whom were married themselves, and who eventually persuaded Wesley to hold more reasonable views—at least for a time.

In August 1748, when John Wesley became ill at Newcastle, he was nursed back to health by Grace Murray, a class leader in the Methodist societies and housekeeper at the Orphan House. Impressed with the kindness and care of Miss Murray, Wesley proposed marriage to her shortly thereafter—she was around thirty years old at the time—though his proposal was, as with his earlier Georgia initiatives, in such vague language that it could easily be misunderstood. At any rate, Grace Murray appreciated the increasing attention, whatever it meant, deemed herself quite fortunate to enjoy the affections of so honorable a man, and accompanied Wesley as he headed south on yet another preaching tour. The busy preacher left Miss Murray at Chinley in what he believed to be the good care of John Bennet.

During the spring and early summer of 1749 Grace Murray traveled with Wesley as he labored in Ireland. In Dublin, the relationship took on a more formal and serious cast in that the couple now entered into a betrothal contract *de praesenti*. The legal status as well as the obligations incurred as a result of such an agreement were often misunderstood.[11] Having entered into this agreement, despite its ambiguity, Wesley sincerely believed that Grace Murray was betrothed to *him* and to no other, but due to a number of factors, some of which were clearly beyond Wesley's control, the agreement was never fulfilled. Indeed, the same sort of hesitancy, misdirection, and even outright confusion that played out in Georgia, a real comedy of errors, would be repeated on English soil.

After the newly engaged couple returned to England, Grace Murray revealed that she had affection for and emotional ties to John Bennet, the preacher in whose care Wesley had left her earlier. Suffering "a piercing conviction of ...inseparable loss," Wesley decided to remove himself from the apparent love triangle, but Miss Murray would not hear of it. "How can you think I love any one better than I love you!" she cried. "I love you a thousand times better than I ever loved John Bennet in my life." But she added, while professing her love for John Wesley, an indication of why she might eventually marry Bennet: "I am afraid, if I don't marry him, he'll run mad."[12]

Concerned about this rival to his designs for marriage, Wesley pointedly asked Grace Murray in September 1749, "Which will you choose?" And once more she professed her love. "I am determined by conscience as well as by inclination, to live and die with you."[13] So anxious was Miss Murray about the possibility of ongoing misunderstanding, of her relationship with Wesley unraveling, that she now urged the reluctant suitor to marry her *immediately*. Wesley, however, could not comply with such a request until he had first satisfied John Bennet, procured consent from his brother Charles, and informed his preachers and societies of his intentions.

Enjoying the gifts of married life since April 1749, when he took Sarah Gwynne as his bride, it is surprising that Charles Wesley was strongly opposed to the possibility that his brother might marry. According to some reports, Charles believed that Miss Murray was already engaged to John Bennet, and he wanted to prevent a scandal as well as to eliminate the gossip that was already beginning to emerge. Or perhaps Charles thought that if John married a servant, that is, someone below his station in life, he would invariably bring discredit to the Methodist movement. Whatever his motivation, Charles Wesley headed for Hindley Hill, persuaded Miss Murray to accompany him to Newcastle, and saw to it that she married John Bennet about a week later. John Wesley was stunned. "Since I was six years old," he exclaimed, "I never met with such a severe trial as for some days past."[14] Perhaps experiencing some guilt over his action, Charles self-righteously intoned upon meeting his brother again, "I renounce all intercourse with you but what I would have with a heathen man or a publican."[15] Relations with Charles continued to be strained over the next couple of years so deep was the hurt that had been inflicted. Likewise, John Wesley's friendship with Mr. Bennet deteriorated until the latter finally repudiated all connection with Wesley, crying "popery, popery"—perhaps a theological veil for a deeper personal hurt.

Having failed so painfully in love on two occasions, and holding some very negative views on the value of marriage itself for the earnest and sincere Christian, it is a wonder that Wesley, so shortly after the Grace Murray fiasco, was contemplating marriage again—and yet it was so. Through his friendship with the Perronets, Wesley became acquainted with Mary Vazeille, a widow of a London trader and woman of considerable means. During the summer of 1750, while Wesley was in Ireland, he wrote to this middle-aged woman though his interest at the time was clearly pastoral not romantic. By the fall, however, Wesley began to think of her as a possible wife. Among other things, he was impressed with Mary's "indefatigable industry, your exact frugality, your uncommon neatness and cleanness both in your person, your clothes and all things round you."[16] Beyond this, Wesley perhaps took special note that Mary was past childbearing years and so his ongoing ministry would not be fettered by the demands and responsibilities of family life.

Shortly before his marriage to Vazeille, Wesley actually urged the preachers under his care who were single to remain so. Despite such counsel, Wesley made the claim to Vincent Perronet that his own impending marriage was appropriate, even called for, by maintaining that he could be more useful to God in a married state than in a single one. Mary Vazeille, in other words, due to her various gifts and graces, would actually aid his ministry, not detract from it. In fact, Wesley informed his wife shortly after their marriage, which took place either on February 18 or 19, 1751 (though perhaps he should have informed her *before* the marriage), not only that he wanted "to crowd all your life with the work of faith and the labour of love,"[17] but also that "if I thought I should [preach one sermon, or travel one mile the less on that account] my dear, as well as I love you, I would never see your face [any] more."[18]

At first Wesley's marriage was good, even affectionate. His letters to his wife were marked by both attentiveness and love. In March, for example, Wesley wrote, "I can imagine then I am sitting just by you, and see and hear you all the while, softly speak and sweetly smile."[19] The following month he lifted Mary's spirits by relating, "Last night I had the pleasure of receiving two letters from my dearest earthly friend."[20] And in another letter that same month Wesley wrote, "How is it that absence does not lessen but increase my affection? I feel you every day nearer to my heart. O that God may continue his unspeakable gift."[21] In May 1751, in a very romantic perhaps even mawkish way, Wesley observed, "Love is talkative. Therefore I can't wait any longer. For it is two weeks since I wrote the former."[22]

However, as letters were the vehicles for sustaining Wesley's marriage, for expressing kindness and affection, at least early on, they were also the means that actually helped to despoil his relationship with Mary Wesley. Exercising what can best be described as poor judgment, Wesley gave his wife permission, shortly after their marriage, to open all of his correspondence: "If any letter comes to you directed to the Rev. Mr. John Wesley, open it: it is for yourself."[23] Exercising this liberty, Mrs. Wesley came to realize that her husband was corresponding with several women. In 1757, for example, Wesley was writing to Dorothy Furly, Sarah Crosby, and Sarah Ryan, among others. It was a letter to this last woman which would cause so much trouble.

As one who frequented Methodist services, Sarah Ryan was converted under John Wesley's ministry at Spitalfields in 1754 and was made the housekeeper at Kingswood a few years later. Ryan's placement in such a position drew criticism from both friends and foes alike, since she had married three men before this appointment—though she was currently living alone—and had not always taken the trouble to divorce one before she married another. Mrs. Wesley undoubtedly thought little of this housekeeper and resented the attention that her husband paid her. At a conference in Bristol, where Ryan was presiding at dinner with Wesley, Mrs. Wesley, in a fit of jealous anger, burst into the room and informed the guests that "the whore now serving you has three husbands living."[24] Mary's relationship with her husband deteriorated even further when, in searching his pockets, she discovered an endearing letter from him to Sarah Ryan in January 1758. The language of the letter breathed an air of affection and perhaps even of deep emotional ties between the correspondents—ties that would give pause to almost any spouse: "The conversing with you, either by speaking or writing, is an unspeakable blessing to me. I cannot think of you without thinking of God. Others often lead me to Him; but it is, as it were, going round about: you bring me straight into His presence."[25]

About a week after this discovery, Mary left John Wesley vowing she would never return, though she came back after only a couple of days. This was to be the first of a series of departures in an increasingly sour relationship. Astonished and saddened by this turn of events, Wesley reflected over the appropriateness of this letter and of his correspondence with Mrs. Ryan in general, and he concluded, in a rather self-assured way, that he had, after all, done well. Once this judgment was made, Wesley simply viewed the entire affair under the larger principle that he had the right, as he put it, "of conversing with whom I please." Unfortunately, such a viewpoint failed to take into account Mary Wesley's perspective, her painful estimate of things.

Just how did matters appear to Mary Wesley? For one thing, she was married to a man who often neglected her in the name of service to God: "Molly, let us make the best of life. Oh for zeal! I want to be on the full stretch for God!"[26] And though Wesley was not willing to preach one sermon less in a married state than in a single one, he was apparently very willing to spend considerable time with women other than his wife—under the banner of ministry of course—in both conversation and in letter writing. Time spent, whether in ministry or not, surely bespeaks of valuation, and Mary Wesley quickly got the message.

And then there were Wesley's deprecating views on marriage itself expressed from time to time, his counsel to his single preachers, and even hints about the intimacy, or the lack thereof, in his own marriage. Add to all this Wesley's description of the nature of his marriage early on, spoken of in terms of the innocence of angels—"Undoubtedly it is the will of God that we should be as guardian angels to each other. O what an union is that whereby we are united! The resemblance even of that between Christ and his Church!"[27]—and the picture that begins to emerge, here offered as a cautious suggestion, is that perhaps Wesley and his wife were engaged in a continent marriage, if not from the beginning of their union, then at least at the present. If continence does depict the nature of Wesley's marital relationship, if Wesley continued to fear the specter of loving the creature more than the Creator, if his ascetic bent went this far, then this would go a long way in explaining Mary Wesley's concern, even jealousy, over her husband's other relationships with women. Neglected in many ways, Mary Wesley would naturally hunger for what affection and intimacy Wesley was evidently giving to others, Sarah Ryan in particular.

The strain of Wesley's faltering marriage was bad enough, and few can doubt the perplexities of his personal life, but during this period he also bore the considerable pressure, on a professional level, of being repeatedly criticized for his "aberrant" church practices, the ongoing employment of lay preachers in particular. In 1748, in response to an attack by a clergyperson on his preachers, Wesley wryly replied, "Will you condemn such a preacher, because he has not learning or has not a university education? What then? He saves those sinners from their sins whom the man of learning and education cannot save."[28] And several years later, Wesley considered what advantages could be had from a liberal education, relating the whole matter to *scriptural* Christianity, when he offered his own censure of a gentleman who was deemed by many to be "a religious man": "What a proof of the Fall," Wesley exclaimed. "Even with all the advantages of a liberal education, this person, I will be bold to say, knows just as much of heart religion, of scriptural Christianity, the religion of love, as a child three years old of algebra."[29]

As early as the latter part of the 1740s Wesley's thoughts on ministry had already undergone significant change. Forsaking the kind of ecclesiastical intolerance that had caused him to refuse to baptize a child (because its mother would not have it dipped) or that had denied communion to a deeply pious man, Mr. Bolzius, because he had not been baptized by one in "the apostolic succession," Wesley now focused his thought on the needs of the gospel itself, on the dictates of the evangel, and he acted accordingly: "I think he is a true, evangelical minister...a servant of Christ and His Church," Wesley wrote, "who...so ministers, as to save souls from death, to reclaim sinners from their sins; and that every Christian, if he is able to do it, has authority to save a dying soul."[30] And a few years later Wesley was so firm in the defense of his preachers that he declared, "If we cannot stop a separation [from the Church of England] without stopping lay preachers, the case is clear, we cannot stop it at all."[31] Moreover, when his own brother Charles had threatened to leave the Methodist Conference if laypeople were allowed to partake in the discussions, John Wesley immediately turned to a friend and remarked, "Give my brother his hat."[32]

When Wesley justified his employment of lay preachers in 1756 to Nicholas Norton, he made an implicit distinction between an "extraordinary ministry" and an "ordinary" one: "I do tolerate unordained persons in preaching the gospel, whereas I do not tolerate them administering the sacraments."[33] Indeed, Wesley made sure that his preachers understood the proper scope, the limits, of their ministry, and he related this whole matter to the advancement of real, scriptural Christianity. "You have one business on earth," Wesley declared to his preachers, "to save souls. Give yourself wholly to this....Pursue the whole of scriptural Christianity."[34]

Despite Wesley's reasoned defense of his lay preachers, criticism from his Anglican colleagues continued to flow. It was maintained by some clergy, for instance, that Methodism with its significant and ever growing infrastructure was causing a division, a schism, in the church. Earlier, Mr. Swindells had urged Wesley to compose a piece (for a certain Mr. E) to demonstrate quite clearly that the Methodists would not leave the church. In response, Wesley penned *A Word to a Methodist* in 1748, a work which underscored Methodist faithfulness to the Church of England. Even after this publication, however, John Bailey accused Wesley of acting "contrary to the commands of my spiritual governors and stab[bing] the Church to the very vitals."[35] Wesley replied to this charge in a letter, drafted in 1750, in which he simply focused, once again, on the issue of doctrine—in this case the doctrine of justification by faith—to the neglect of many other vital concerns among his Anglican peers. But by 1752 even his own brother Charles began to worry. In a letter Charles reminded his brother that their present call was "chiefly to the members of that church wherein we have been brought up,"[36] and that they must "never knowingly or willingly to hear or speak, do, or suffer anything which tends to weaken that union."[37]

To the claim that the Church of England was the true church from which Methodism with its newfangled methods had departed, Wesley replied to Gilbert Boyce in the early 1750s, "I do not think either the Church of England, or the People called Methodists, or any other particular Society under heaven to be the *True Church of Christ*. For that Church is but one, and contains all *true* believers."[38] The distinction between the visible and invisible church implicit here was made explicit a few years later in Wesley's notes on Matthew 22:14: "*Many are called; few chosen—* Many hear; few believe. Yea, many are members of the visible, but few of the invisible Church."[39]

During the 1750s Wesley's "functional" as opposed to "institutional" definition of ministry continued to develop along a number of lines to the consternation of several Anglican clergy. First, as of 1750, Wesley claimed that even baptism was not absolutely necessary to salvation. Writing to Gilbert Boyce, he observed, "You think the mode of baptism is 'necessary to salvation.' I deny that even baptism itself is so. If it were every Quaker must be damned, which I can in no wise believe. I hold nothing to be (strictly speaking) necessary to salvation, but this mind which was in Christ."[40] And toward the end of the decade a woman came away from Wesley's preaching at Newlyn, crying, "Nay, if going to church and sacrament will not *put us to heaven*, I know not what will."[41] Wesley, of course, never deprecated the means of grace in his preaching, but he did stress on numerous occasions that they were, after all, simply the *means* and not the *end* of salvation.

Second, after reading Baxter's *History of the Councils* in 1754, Wesley clearly took issue with the well-worked claim of infallibility for church councils in a way that made him sound similar to Luther and that would surely irk the traditionalists of his own church: "What a company of execrable wretches have they been...who have almost in every age since St. Cyprian taken upon them to govern the Church! How has one Council been perpetually cursing another, and delivering all over to Satan....Surely Mahometanism was let loose to reform the Christians."[42]

Third, due to his emphasis on having the mind of Christ, of being transformed and renewed in sanctifying grace, Wesley criticized mere "orthodoxy," a faith which simply revels in intellectual assent, in correct and exact opinion, but which refuses to engage the tempers of the heart: "Orthodoxy, I say, or right opinion, is but a slender part of religion at best, and sometimes no part at all." "I mean," Wesley added, "if a man be a child of God, holy in heart and life, his right opinions are but the smallest part of his religion."[43]

Finally, to top it all, in this same decade Wesley not only came to the defense of some condemned heretics, but he also surmised that they had actually been real Christians all along. In reading *The General Religion of Christians with regard to Prophecy* in 1750, Wesley concluded, "I was fully convinced of what I had long suspected... that the Montanists in the second and third centuries were real, scriptural Christians."[44] He attributed the downfall of these believers to "dry, formal, orthodox men" who in lacking the gifts of the Spirit decried them in others. Perceptive Anglican clergy would conclude that such criticism was directed at some of their numbers as well.

Matters finally came to a head at the Methodist Conference in 1755 held at Leeds. In this setting, Wesley enjoined his preachers to speak their minds on the question of whether they should leave the Church of England. By the third day of the Conference all were in agreement that whether or not it was lawful to separate, it was "in no ways *expedient.*"[45] Several months later Wesley wrote to Thomas Adam on this very matter: "We are fully convinced that to separate from an Established Church is never lawful but when it is absolutely necessary; and we do not see any such necessity yet."[46] Beyond this, John and Charles Wesley offered even greater assurances to those who were questioning their intentions when at the

1756 Methodist Conference they made a "solemn declaration of our purpose, never to separate from the church."[47] And in 1758 Wesley published "Twelve Reasons against Separating from the Church of England," to allay similar fears. John Wesley had been baptized an Anglican; he was determined to die as one as well.

In terms of his doctrine of the church, Wesley never viewed Methodism in a parochial way either as a faction or as a sect. Instead, he considered it against a much larger backdrop as a reforming impulse within the church in general and within Anglicanism in particular. Informed by the good work of Anthony Horneck and the religious society movement, Wesley desired the Methodists to spread scriptural holiness across the land, the very substance of the Christian faith. To that end, and for its great instructional value, he published the best pieces of practical divinity from the universal church (though heavily weighted toward the English tradition) in *A Christian Library*. This series of writings, which was first published in 1750 in fifty volumes, contained selections from Hooker, Ussher, Laud, Bull, Tillotson, Andrews, Pearson, Taylor, Cudworth, and Beveridge, among others. And in terms of continental piety, Wesley thought it appropriate to reproduce Johann Arndt's *True Christianity*, a work that was not only read by many of the pietists, Spener and Francke among them, but which also helped them in their own efforts at reform.

In November 1753, Wesley became seriously ill (he actually thought he was dying and so he composed an epitaph) and his health was little better in January 1754. Wanting to "redeem the time," and in order to provide additional teaching materials for the Methodists, Wesley worked on his *Notes Upon the New Testament* while he recuperated. Utilizing Bengel's *Gnomen*, Wesley eventually composed a very readable commentary that contained many of the leading themes of Methodism, in particular, the importance of holy love as well as the motif of being a real as opposed to a nominal Christian. To illustrate, in his comments on Matthew 23:31, Wesley identified both the kingdom of God and real Christianity with the inculcation of holy tempers in the heart. He had made a similar association in 1748, in his sermon "Upon Our Lord's Sermon on the Mount, Discourse VI": "He [Christ] has laid before us those dispositions of soul which constitute real Christianity: the inward tempers contained in that holiness 'without which no man shall see the Lord.'"[48]

So important was the motif of real Christianity to Wesley during the 1750s that at some points in his *Notes* he would actually step back from his objectivity as a scholar, so to speak, and directly address his readers. For instance, in his observations on Mark 12:34 ("You are not far from the kingdom" [NRSV]), Wesley wrote, "Reader, art not thou? Then go on: be a real Christian: else it had been better for thee to have been afar off."[49] Likewise, in his comments on Acts 26:28 ("Agrippa said to Paul, 'Are you so quickly persuading me to become a Christian?'" [NRSV]), Wesley cautioned, "Reader, stop not with Agrippa; but go on with Paul."[50] Beyond this, in his explication of Romans 8:15 ("For you did not receive a spirit of slavery to fall back into fear, but you have received a spirit of adoption. When we cry, 'Abba! Father!'" [NRSV]), Wesley clearly distinguished real Christians from those who have received the spirit of bondage, especially when he wrote, "For ye who are real Christians, have not received the spirit of bondage—The Holy Spirit was not properly a spirit of bondage, even in the time of the Old Testament."[51] And finally, in his observations on Matthew 13:28, Wesley made a distinction between outside Christians and open sinners, with implications for real Christianity as well. He observed, "Darnel, in the church, is properly outside Christians, such as have the form of godliness, without the power. Open sinners, such as have neither the form nor the power, are not so properly darnel, as thistles and brambles."[52] And real Christians, it could have been added, have both the *form* and the *power* of religion.

As Wesley developed his thought on real Christianity during the period of 1748–1758, especially in his *Notes*, so too did he consider what constitutes the faith of a servant, of one who "fears God and works righteousness." In his comments on Acts 10:35, for example, Wesley observed:

> But in every nation he that *feareth God and worketh righteousness*—He that, first, reverences God, as great, wise, good, the cause, end, and governor of all things; and secondly, from this awful regard to him, not only avoids all known evil, but endeavours, according to the best light he has, to do all things well; is *accepted of him*—through

Christ, though he knows him not....He is in the favour of God, whether enjoying his written word and ordinances or not. Nevertheless the addition of these is an unspeakable blessing to those who were before in *some measure* accepted.[53]

Note that Wesley refers not simply to Christian lands, but to "every nation." In other words, here he is speaking quite broadly and is highlighting the salutary effects of prevenient and convincing grace. Though these believers neither know Christ, nor are they acquainted with the promises of the gospel in the Bible, and though they are not even familiar with nor do they utilize the ordinances of the church such as the sacraments, and again though they have no assurance that their sins are forgiven in Christ, yet in some measure, in some sense, these believers are accepted. But is this *degree* of acceptance equivalent to justifying, regenerating faith, what Wesley often referred to as real Christianity in his *Notes* and elsewhere? Or did Wesley perhaps during the 1750s repudiate the importance of having the proper Christian faith in favor of a more general faith, of one which "fears God and works righteousness"? The answer to these questions must be "No," in light of the following considerations.

First of all, since 1738, Wesley had taught that regenerating faith grows out of an awareness of God's gracious love for sinners. Indeed, Wesley often quoted 1 John 4:19—"We love because he first loved us"—in order to display just how "faith working by love," salvation properly speaking, is actualized in heart and life. Put another way, Christ is both the source and the object of regenerating faith. Accordingly, the liberty entailed in freedom from the power of sin, the inculcation of *holy* tempers in the heart, the very substance of salvation, does not arise from either prevenient or convincing grace, but only from the initially *sanctifying* grace of the new birth.

Second, if such "fearful" believers ("fearing God and working righteousness," their "awful regard" to God) are not born of God, then neither can they be justified. Indeed, for Wesley, although justification and regeneration can be distinguished logically (the one being the work that God does "for us"; the other what God does "in us"), they yet occur simultaneously in the life of believers. More to the point, these two works of grace must *always* occur together, never one without the other. If believers were not born of God and were therefore still under the power of sin, then neither could they be justified in this *ongoing* practice of sin. During this period, then, as he had earlier, Wesley taught quite clearly that justification pertains to those sins "which are *past*," not to the ongoing practice of sin. Severing the new birth from justification, then, can only result in antinomianism, the undermining of *holiness*.

Yet during the 1750s, in a very pastoral way, Wesley wanted to underscore that the sincere believers depicted in Acts 10:35 have an important measure of grace (prevenient) and therefore are not to be discouraged as they approach redemption, properly speaking. Giving evidence of this sensibility late in his career (1788), Wesley wrote to Melville Horne, "When fifty years ago my brother Charles and I, in the simplicity of our hearts, told the good people of England that unless they *knew* their sins were forgiven, they were under the wrath and curse of God, I marvel...that they did not stone us!"

What Wesley and his brother had learned in the interim and what was in place even during the 1750s was the notion that there is, after all, an intermediate state between a child of God and a child of the devil and that those who are not assured that their sins are forgiven may have a degree of faith and, therefore, may be admitted to the Lord's Supper.[54] With such a distinction in place, Wesley could be more pastorally sensitive and not discourage those whom God has not discouraged, while at the same time he maintained his relatively high standards with respect to what he called real, proper, scriptural Christianity. Wesley held both of these elements together in his energetic and extensive ministry, to the bewilderment of some of his colleagues, but to the good of others, chiefly the poor. The word, then, to all earnest seekers, whether justified or not, at any point along the way of salvation, was ever to go forward, to improve the rich grace of God. To this noble end, Wesley dedicated his efforts; to this lofty goal, he labored in service.

7

Challenges Without and Within

Though Wesley could make the case that Methodism was doctrinally orthodox, in step with historical Anglicanism and the broader church, it was becoming increasingly difficult during the 1760s to contend that Methodism had not departed from the ecclesiastical law of the Church of England. For one thing, some of Wesley's lay preachers were no longer content with simply preaching and had taken it upon themselves to administer the Lord's Supper. Paul Greenwood, Thomas Mitchell, and John Murlin, preachers at Norwich, all officiated at the sacrament. Upon learning of such a presumptuous action, Charles Wesley was naturally incensed and urged his brother to end this practice. John, too, was greatly concerned and took measures to reassure his brother that effective discipline would be put into place.

Wesley was doing all that he could to maintain good order within Methodism, but his unswerving commitment to fostering the work of the gospel was invariably pushing his polity beyond the bounds of the Anglican sense of propriety. Earlier, in 1746, Wesley had read Lord Peter King's work *An Enquiry into the Constitution, Discipline, Unity, and Worship of the Primitive Church,* and in 1755 he perused Edward Stillingfleet's *Irenicon.* In the former work, King championed the notion that the office of elders and bishops in the early church was of the same order, though different in degree. For his part, Stillingfleet, the Bishop of Worcester, agreed with King that bishops and presbyters in the early church were essentially the same, but he went on to repudiate the notion that Christ had prescribed any particular form of church polity, episcopal or not. Such views emboldened Wesley to respond to the Earl of Dartmouth in April 1761 that Bishop Stillingfleet had convinced the Methodists that their earlier view—that none but episcopal ordination is valid—was "an entire mistake."[1]

Though such reasoning with respect to polity and governance should have led Wesley to ordain lay preachers to the office of priest, thereby enabling them to administer the sacraments, he hesitated during 1765 when his need for laborers was especially great. Instead, and in a highly irregular manner, Wesley sought the services of a Greek bishop. After examining the bishop's credentials and being fully satisfied, Wesley allowed this Greek cleric, who could hardly speak a word of English, to ordain John Jones and later six others. Wesley defended his actions to the printer of *St. James Chronicle* in 1765, but he would have second thoughts. The issue of illegitimacy, he began to think, turned not on the authority of the Greek bishop, but on the fact that the ordinations had been "procured by money and performed in an unknown tongue."[2]

As an overseer in the church, responsible for the good order of the Methodist societies laced throughout England and Ireland, Wesley bore the burden of seeing to it that suitable laborers would be supplied to continue the work of the gospel. And though Wesley, himself, obviously was not willing to ordain anyone during the mid 1760s, his commitment both to field preaching by clergy and to the employment of lay preachers was by now nonnegotiable. A letter to Charles Wesley in June 1760 had posed the basic dilemma: "Leave preaching or leave the Church."[3] Wesley, not wishing to leave either, could only respond that "we have reason to thank God it is not come to this yet."[4] And though it may look as if Wesley were equivocating at this point, he was actually already quite firm in his views. In fact, in a letter to the Earl of Dartmouth in April 1761, he reasoned that "if there is a law that a minister of Christ who is not suffered to preach the gospel in the church should not preach it elsewhere, I do judge that law to be absolutely sinful."[5] And of the value of field preaching itself Wesley noted in 1764, "What can shake Satan's kingdom like field preaching."[6] The following year he added, "So plain it is that field-preaching is the most effectual way of overturning Satan's kingdom."[7] In light of these and other pronouncements, come what may, Wesley was not about to put aside this gracious instrument of the gospel.

In 1762, William Warburton, Bishop of Gloucester, published *The*

Office and Operations of the Holy Spirit Vindicated from the Insults of Infidelity and the Abuses of Fanaticism, a work critical of Wesley and the Methodists. Demonstrating a measure of fair play, Warburton submitted this piece to Wesley before it was published, and the latter returned it after having corrected its false readings, improper glosses, and other errors. Once the essay was made public, however, Wesley set aside a few days, November 26-29, to draft a more lengthy response.

Among other things, Warburton maintained that the Methodists were fanatics because they claimed to enjoy operations of the Holy Spirit that were reserved, in the bishop's judgment, for the apostolic age. In his detailed reply, Wesley pointed out that he and the Methodists did not "pretend to any extraordinary measure of the Spirit,"[8] but only to what could be claimed by every Christian minister. Putting aside dreams, visions, and revelations as being of a doubtful or disputable nature, Wesley instead focused on the operations of the Spirit as the "Guide of truth" who enlightens the understanding, as "the Comforter who purifies and supports the will," and as the One who now "hears and answers prayer even beyond the ordinary course of nature."[9] But Wesley also wanted to make clear to the bishop that the ministry of the Spirit could be distinguished from the course of nature in terms of both effectiveness and time. "I have seen very many persons," Wesley stated, "changed in a moment from the spirit of fear, horror, despair, to the spirit of love, joy and praise."[10] And it was, in reality, the efficacy of the Spirit, and the profession of such by the Methodists, that Warburton found so troubling.

Sensing that Warburton's objections were actually aimed not at fanaticism but at real, scriptural Christianity, Wesley steered the dispute in that direction:

> And what use is it of, what good end does it serve, to term England a Christian country? Although it is true most of the natives are called Christians, have been baptized, frequent the ordinances; and although here and there a *real* Christian is to be found, "as a light shining in a dark place,"—does it do any honour to our great Master among those who are not called by His name? Does it recommend Christianity to the Jews, the Mahometans, or the avowed heathens? Surely no one can conceive it does.[11]

To be sure, Wesley maintained that "every true Christian" receives the Holy Spirit as Paraclete or Comforter, as "the Spirit of all truth," and as the anointing mentioned in 1 John, one of Wesley's favorite books of the Bible on this theme.[12] And just in case Warburton might miss the thrust of these rebuttals, Wesley offered him a question to ponder: "If men are not Christians till they are renewed after the image of Christ, and if the people of England in general are not thus renewed, why do we term them so?"[13] The original question of fanaticism had now become what constitutes the proper Christian faith. Wesley had turned the tables on the good bishop.

It would be a mistake, however, to conclude that Wesley's more important letters and theological pieces were simply *responses* to various persons (or groups) who differed from the Methodists—such as Warburton in the present or Bishop Gibson earlier. At times Wesley initiated the discussion, especially when he believed an important truth of the gospel was at stake. Such was the case in 1762 when he wrote one of his more forceful and energetic theological pieces, "A Blow at the Root or Christ Stabbed in the House of His Friends."

From his vantage point in eighteenth-century England, Wesley looked out toward the Christian community, toward Catholicism and Protestantism alike, and saw all the elements of antinomianism, that is, beliefs that undermine the very importance of *being* holy. Of Roman Catholics, for example, he opined in his "Blow at the Root" that "they found out another way to get to heaven without holiness...they substituted penances, pilgrimages, praying to saints and angels; and, above all these, masses for the dead, absolution by a Priest, and extreme unction," for the cruciality of holy love. Of Protestants, Wesley observed, "How shall they hope to see God, without holiness? Why, by doing no harm, doing good, going to the church and sacrament. And many thousands sit down content with this, believing they are in the high road to heaven."[14] Even more emphatically, he declared, "They [Protestants] well know, that although none can be a real Christian, without carefully abstaining from all evil, using every means of grace at every opportunity, and doing all possible good to all men; yet a man may go this far...and be but an Heathen still."[15]

Many Calvinists thought that "Blow at the Root" was directed principally at them, and there was a growing air of uneasiness between the Methodists and Calvinists during this period. Earlier, James Hervey had decided to be more forthright concerning the truths of predestination, election, and imputation. To that end he drafted *Theron and Aspasio* and asked Wesley for his comments. When Wesley returned the manuscript with his suggestions, Hervey complained, "You are not my friend, if you do not take more liberty with me."[16] Wesley complied with this request, offered more serious criticisms, and thereby greatly offended the author. Among other things he suggested that some of Hervey's notions were not scriptural and especially took exception to Hervey's idea of imputation since it could render believers content, even self-satisfied, without holiness. Deeply concerned, Wesley published "A Preservative Against Unsettled Notions of Religion" (1758) as a brief rebuttal and later, after Hervey's death, "Thoughts on the Imputed Righteousness of Christ."

Chafing under this censure, Hervey wrote a number of private letters very critical of Wesley's views. However, when his health began to fail in 1758, Hervey had second thoughts about publishing this material and from his deathbed specifically ordered his brother *not* to print the letters. Somehow the material fell into the hands of William Cudworth, an unscrupulous preacher, who quickly published it. Hervey's brother, William, noticed a number of errors in the manuscript that reflected badly on his brother, and so violating his promise not to publish, he came forward with a "corrected" edition of the work in 1765, "Eleven Letters from the late Rev. Mr. Hervey to the Rev. Mr. John Wesley; containing an Answer to that Gentleman's Remarks on *Theron and Aspasio.*" "The Lord Our Righteousness" was Wesley's quick response. In this sermon, he maintained that the work of Christ was the meritorious rather than the formal cause of salvation, a view which allowed for prevenience, free will, and universal redemption and which consequently undermined the Calvinist notions of predestination and irresistible grace.[17] So significant was the publication of this sermon that Albert Outler has noted "It signals the end of Wesley's efforts to avoid an open rift with the Calvinists; it signals the beginning of that stage in his career…labelled 'the later Wesley.'"[18]

Though by the mid 1760s Wesley could no longer avoid an open rift with the Calvinists—albeit the real struggle was yet to come—his relations with George Whitefield were actually improving. In January 1766, Whitefield visited Wesley breathing "nothing but peace and love."[19] The following year Wesley observed, with much gratitude, that "God has indeed effectually broken down the wall of partition which was between us."[20] Thus, though each leader continued to articulate a very different theology, each was also fully aware of the great work of God being accomplished by the other. And in 1769, shortly before Whitefield's death, Wesley took note on more than one occasion of an agreeable and profitable time spent with this magnificent but by then worn out preacher.[21]

Wesley's relationship with his wife, Mary, had also improved by the mid 1760s though there had been considerable misunderstanding and tension between the couple. In 1759, Wesley had complained in a letter to Ebenezer Blackwell that Mary had picked his lock, stolen some of his papers, and showed them to several people, some of whom were his Calvinist detractors.[22] To address this issue, Wesley detailed ten items that he found reproachable in his wife's behavior, in a lengthy letter to her dated October 23, 1759. "I dislike the not being safe in my own house," Wesley complained. "My house is *not* my castle. I cannot call even my study, even my bureau, my own. They are liable to be plundered every day."[23]

Continually insisting on *his* freedom, Wesley requested that Mary "let me go where I please and to whom I please without giving an account to any."[24] And in a subsequent letter in March 1760, Wesley reminded his wife of her marital vows and the promise of obedience: "This must be your indispensable duty," Wesley declared. "Till then I have the same right to claim obedience from you as you have to claim it from [your son] Noah Vazeille."[25] A year later, Wesley was utterly frustrated with his wife's thefts and so "finding all other means ineffectual...I opened my wife's bureau and took what I found of my own."[26] But shortly after this episode, the fever broke, so to speak, and by 1763 Wesley's relationship with his wife had significantly improved—at least for a while. On January 5, 1763, writing to his brother Charles, Wesley observed with great satisfaction, "My wife gains ground. She is quite peaceable and loving *to all.*"[27] The following year, in a letter to Ann Foard, Wesley actually praised his wife and remarked that *her* strong faith profited him exceedingly.[28] And in 1766, Wesley again wrote to Charles and remarked that his wife "continues in amazing temper...not one jarring string."[29]

Despite these improved relations, Wesley still could not see how his own behavior, in particular his valuations and judgments with respect to ministry, would inevitably lead to further strains in his marriage. A few years later, in August 1768, while Wesley was on a preaching tour, Mary Wesley became seriously ill. Upon learning of his wife's poor condition, Wesley immediately set out for the Foundery in London where Mary was staying, but he remained at her sickbed for only one hour once he had determined that her fever had gone down. The ever dutiful minister then set out for Bristol to more work and more ministry. In a letter to his wife the next month, Wesley reflected on this incident and made a very telling comparison: "I remember when it was my own case at this very place," he wrote, "and when you spared no pains in nursing and waiting upon me, till it pleased God to make you the chief instrument of restoring my strength."[30] Mary, in other words, had provided tender care, had actually *nursed* John. Wesley, on the other hand, saw fit to spend very little time at Mary's side, even when she was very ill. And though he was admittedly heading for the Methodist Conference in Bristol, which would take place two days later on Tuesday, August 16, this does not justify remaining at the Foundery for only an hour. The schedule was not that tight. Once again, Mary got the message.

It was during this period of relative calm in his marriage that Wesley published some of his more important pieces on the process of sanctification in general and of Christian perfection in particular. In 1763, for instance, in the sermon "On Sin in Believers," he clearly distinguished between the *guilt, power,* and *being* of sin and thereby underscored the deliverance entailed in perfect love. "The *guilt* is one thing, the *power* another, and the *being* yet another. That believers [justified and regenerated] are delivered from the *guilt* and *power* of sin we allow; that they are delivered from the *being* of it we deny."[31] Moreover, in 1765, Wesley published a summary sermon, "The Scripture Way of Salvation," which represented some of his best thinking about the flow of redemption and of Christian perfection—and all of it presented in a very orderly and coherent fashion. The following year, Wesley brought forth his classic on the subject, *A Plain Account of Christian Perfection,* which presented his understanding of perfect love from his initial insights in 1725 to his more nuanced thought of the present.

During the early 1760s Wesley repeatedly proclaimed from the pulpit, and at times from the fields of both England and Ireland, the importance of "going on to perfection." In November 1761 in London, for example, he preached a series of sermons on perfect love. The response was gratifying. In a letter to Alexander Coates that same year Wesley defined Christian perfection as "loving God with all the heart; receiving Christ as Prophet, Priest, and King, to reign alone over all our thoughts, words, and actions."[32] The following year, in a letter to his brother Charles, he underscored the salience of humility and patience in this rich actualization of grace: "By perfection I mean the humble, gentle, patient love of God and man ruling all the tempers, words, and actions, the whole heart and the whole life."[33] As to the manner of perfection, Wesley believed that it is always "wrought in the soul by faith, by a simple act of faith; consequently in an instant."[34] He then added, to clarify, "But I believe a gradual work both preceding and following that instant."[35]

Though Wesley explored the subject of Christian perfection to the consternation of the Calvinist Methodists such as Walter Shirley and the Countess of Huntingdon—who, by the way, were much more pessimistic in terms of what the grace of God could *realize* in the Christian life—Wesley nevertheless avoided the term "sinless perfection" not only because it was unscriptural, but also because it might lead some to believe that those who were entirely sanctified were free even from involuntary transgressions of the law of love, a clear impossibility in this life. That is, those who love God with all their hearts, who have the mind which was in Christ Jesus, are free from willfully violating a known law of God—as are all the sons and daughters of God—but beyond this they are free from the *being* of sin, the carnal nature, as well. Despite such liberty, those whose hearts are pure are not and can never be free from involuntary transgressions of the law of love as well as from the infirmities (dullness of mind, confusion of judgment, etc.) which ever pertain to the human condition. By the end of the decade, Wesley defined Christian Perfection quite simply to an Irish woman as loving God with all our heart, being entirely devoted to God, regaining the whole image of God, having all the mind that was in Christ, and walking as Christ had walked.[36]

It was also during the decade of the 1760s that Wesley had become firmly convinced that the Methodist revival would not prosper unless his preachers proclaimed the importance of "going on to perfection." In 1765, he examined the Methodist society at Bristol and was surprised to learn that it had fifty fewer members than during his previous visit. Wesley attributed this decline to the failure to preach Christian perfection forthrightly. In fact, wherever Christian perfection was not proclaimed, Wesley reasoned, "be the preachers ever so eloquent, there is little increase, either in the number or grace of the hearers."[37] Writing to George Merryweather in February 1766, Wesley noted that "where Christian perfection is not strongly and explicitly preached, there is seldom any remarkable blessing from God, and consequently little addition to the Society."[38] Even more emphatically, Wesley wrote on one occasion, "Till you press the believers to expect *full salvation* now you must not look for any revival."[39] So concerned was Wesley with the ongoing proclamation of Christian perfection that in preparing for the upcoming Methodist Conference in August 1767, he opined that "it will be determined whether all our preachers or none shall continually *insist* upon Christian perfection."[40]

For Wesley, then, the Christian life was understood in a dynamic, not static, way. The realization of the grace of God in the human heart ever beckoned one toward deeper appropriations of grace. Writing to John Fletcher in 1768, Wesley observed, "I seldom find it profitable for me to converse with any who are not athirst for perfection and who are not big with earnest expectation of receiving it every moment."[41] That same year, in a letter to his brother, Wesley pointed out that he was at the end of his wits in terms of two matters: the church and Christian perfection. "Unless both you and I stand in the gap *in good earnest,*" Wesley warned, "the

Methodists will drop them both. Talking will not avail. We must do, or be borne away."[42] A year later, Wesley continued to express concern in this area. "I think it is high time that you and I at least should come to a point. Shall we go on in asserting perfection against all the world? Or shall we quietly let it drop?"[43]

Despite the reluctance of some of his preachers, Wesley was encouraged during the 1760s with numerous testimonies of perfect love among the members of the Methodist societies. In a letter to Sarah Crosby in 1761, for instance, he affirmed that "five in one band received a second blessing."[44] The following year, Wesley related to Samuel Furly that he had encountered forty or fifty people who declare that "He has enabled me to give Him all my heart," a witness that Wesley did not doubt since, as he put it, "I can take their word, for I know them well."[45] In Manchester, in 1762, Wesley observed that there were sixty-three who believed that God had "cleansed their hearts."[46] And in Otley during June 1764, Wesley took great care to examine those who believed they had been saved from all sin.[47]

A good indication of the number of witnesses to Christian perfection at this time is revealed in Wesley's letter to his brother Charles in 1766, in which he noted, "That perfection which I believe, I can boldly preach, because I think I see five hundred witnesses of it."[48] Surrounded by such testimonies, and though in 1768 he related in a letter to Lawrence Coughlan that he had taught perfection "these forty years," Wesley himself never gave testimony to this richest actualization of grace. "I have told all the world I am not perfect....I have not attained the character I draw."[49] Still Wesley was firm in his belief of the appropriateness of both teaching and preaching this doctrine—because of the "cloud of witnesses" testifying to it and, more important, because of the clear testimony of Scripture: "This perfection cannot be a delusion," Wesley declared, "unless the Bible be a delusion too."[50]

Wesley's example of preaching the doctrine of Christian perfection in a tempered and judicious way was unfortunately not followed by all of his preachers. George Bell, for instance, who had been converted in 1758 and was subsequently associated with Thomas Maxfield and John Wesley at the Foundery, preached Christian perfection in London and peppered his sermons with screaming and with wild gesticulations from the pulpit. His "perfection" was frankly antinomian: free from rule, precept, and good judgment. Indeed, so fanatical was Bell that he actually believed he had a miraculous power to discern the spirits, and he sharply condemned his opponents—mistaking them for the enemies of God—on this basis.[51] Hearing several disturbing reports, Wesley investigated the whole matter, and after meeting with Mr. Bell in December 1762 and realizing that there would be no change in his behavior, expelled this ranting preacher from his leadership role in the London societies of West Street and the Foundery. The following month Wesley met with Bell again and tried to convince him, in a very pastoral way, of his numerous mistakes, the latest one being the teaching that the world would end on February 28 of that year. After this meeting, which did not go well, George Bell and those associated with him, including John Dixon, Joseph Calvert, and Benjamin Biggs, quit the Methodist society and renounced all fellowship with John Wesley.

Thomas Maxfield, a friend of Bell's, was similarly caught up in the controversy. Maxfield was the preacher Susanna Wesley had recommended to her son back in 1740. Now, more then twenty years later, Wesley was no longer satisfied with Maxfield's ministry, in particular his deprecation of justification (teaching that a justified person is not born of God) and his repudiation of instantaneous entire sanctification. In October 1762, Wesley wrote to rebuke his erring disciple. "You have over and over denied instantaneous sanctification to *me*. But I have known and taught it (and so has my brother, as our writings show) above these twenty years."[52]

So disruptive was the ministry of Maxfield that a division emerged in some of the London societies. Mrs. Coventry, for example, threw down her class ticket and those of her husband, daughters, and servants and proclaimed that she would "hear two doctrines no longer....Mr. Maxfield preached *perfection,* but Mr. Wesley pulled it down."[53] John Wesley's reply was quick and to the point. "So I did, that perfection of Benjamin Harris, G. Bell, and all who abetted them."[54] By March 1763, Maxfield had actually excluded himself from the Methodist pulpit by refusing to preach at the Foundery. "[And] so the breach is made," Wesley declared.[55]

But the damage had already been done. "They [Bell and Maxfield] made the very name of Perfection stink in the nostrils," Wesley wrote, "even of those who loved and honoured it before."[56] That same year Maxfield became an independent minister in London, severing all connection with John Wesley.

The Bell-Maxfield fiasco convinced Wesley that greater care and discipline had to be exercised in terms of *what* was preached from a Methodist pulpit. To that end, the Methodist Conference of 1763 adopted the Model Deed and inserted it into the *Minutes*. This document established a crucial standard of doctrine for preachers in terms of John Wesley's *Explanatory Notes upon the New Testament* and his four volumes of sermons. In this way, Wesley hoped to bring greater order and stability to the ongoing life of Methodism.

As Wesley articulated the doctrine of Christian perfection more carefully in the face of many witnesses, he further reflected on the importance of real Christianity and the whole matter of assurance. In 1760, he stated that the very design of the Oxford Methodists was "to forward each other in true, scriptural Christianity,"[57] and in 1769 he revealed to Joseph Benson that "when I was at Oxford, I never was afraid of any but the almost Christians."[58] Moreover, the distinction between nominal and real Christianity was beginning to take on a paradigmatic flavor such that Wesley now began to speak not only of half Christians but also of half Methodists! To Lady Maxwell he commented in 1764, "And I entreat you do not regard the half-Methodists—if we must use the name. Do not mind them who endeavour to hold Christ in one hand and the world in the other. I want you to be all a Christian."[59] Beyond this, Wesley's letters to Ann Bolton in 1768 and a later one in 1770 illustrate the ongoing theme that the faith of a servant, though earnest and virtuous, yet falls short of the promises which pertain to all real Christians. "I am glad you are *still waiting* for the kingdom of God," Wesley wrote to Bolton, "although as yet you are rather in the state of a servant than of a child."[60]

In the mid 1750s, Wesley had written to Richard Tompson and clarified his doctrine of assurance in two key respects: on the one hand, he argued that there is an intermediate state between a child of the devil and a child of God such that those who are not assured that their sins are forgiven may have a degree of faith and, therefore, may be admitted to the Lord's Supper.[61] On the other hand, Wesley continued to emphasize the importance of assurance for the Christian faith, asserting, "But still I believe the *proper* Christian faith which purifies the heart implies such a conviction."[62] Here Wesley pointed out with regard to assurance that "the whole Christian Church in the first centuries enjoyed it."[63] He exclaimed, "If that knowledge were destroyed, or wholly *withdrawn*, I could not then say, I had *Christian* faith."[64] More to the point, in his summary sermon "The Scripture Way of Salvation" (1765), he actually linked saving faith with assurance by maintaining "it is certain this [saving] faith necessarily implies an *assurance* . . . that 'Christ loved *me*, and gave himself for *me*.'"[65]

Wesley's subsequent letters to Richard Tompson contained further clarification on this topic and one significant, though seldom understood, exception. Concerning this last point, Wesley admitted to Mr. Tompson on February 18, 1756, in a way reminiscent of the 1745 and 1747 conferences, that one may be in a state of justification and yet lack assurance. These are what Wesley called "the exempt cases" or "exceptions." Thus, in response to the question "Can a man who has not a clear assurance that his sins are forgiven be in a state of justification?" Wesley affirmed, "I believe there are *some* instances of it."[66] However, it was not until now, the 1760s, that Wesley indicated *the reason* for this exception. In 1768 he wrote to Dr. Rutherforth:

> Yet I do not affirm there are no exceptions to this general rule [of the association of a measure of assurance with justification]. Possibly some may be in the favour of God, and yet go mourning all the day long. But I believe this is usually owing either to disorder of body or ignorance of the gospel promises.[67]

On the one hand, the elderly Wesley still did not identify or confuse the faith of a servant, and its measure of acceptance, with the assurance that one's sins are forgiven; being under "the spirit of bondage," a servant, properly speaking, lacks justifying faith. On the other hand, Wesley recognized that in some exceptional cases those who are justified and regenerated (and hence children of God) may lack an assurance that their sins are forgiven due to either ignorance or bodily disorder.[68] This means, then, that Wesley actually defined the phrase "the faith of a servant" in at least two key ways: The first, which is a broad[69] usage and which occurs repeatedly in Wesley's writings, *excludes* justification, regeneration, and assurance and corresponds to the spirit of bondage, noted earlier. The second, which is a narrow usage and which seldom occurs, corresponds to the exempt cases and exceptions noted, and it *includes* justification and regeneration but not assurance. Interestingly, although the faith of a servant in this second sense is obviously Christian (saving) faith since it includes justification and regeneration, Wesley still did not refer to it as the *proper* Christian faith since it lacks assurance.

With these distinctions in place, Wesley's theology was then able to face one of the more thoroughgoing criticisms directed at it by a subsequent age, namely, that his pastoral notion of a positive evaluation of the faith of a servant, of one "who fears God and works righteousness," in reality placed his theology well beyond the bounds of historical Anglicanism and the doctrine of justification by *faith* in particular. For example, Lord Acton (John Emerich Edward Dalberg), the famous nineteenth-century British historian and philosopher and Regius Professor of Modern History at Cambridge University, maintained that the crucial date in the relation of Wesley to the Church of England was December 1, 1767, when Wesley entered in his Journal, "We must get rid of long words and simply fall back on the truth that he that feareth God and doeth righteousness is accepted of him."[70] Lord Acton contended quite vigorously that "this date rather than 1784 marks the separation of Methodism from the Church of England."[71]

What Acton failed to realize, however, was that just as Wesley did not understand the "faith of a servant" in a monolithic way, but in a twofold way, so too did he understand the phrase "fear God and worketh righteousness" in a similar fashion. As we saw in chapter 6, Wesley employed this phrase—as he commented on Acts 10:35—in a very broad way, which embraced many people from distant lands and faiths, but which did not *necessarily* include justification and the new birth. This broad usage was also reflected in Wesley's boast that he did *not* require the testimony of justification, the new birth or the chronicling of a conversion experience in order for one to join the Methodists. All that was necessary was simply a "desire to flee the wrath which is to come." More important for the task at hand, Wesley expressed this very same sentiment using his idiom "fearing God and working righteousness," indicating quite clearly that the broad use of this phrase was identified neither with the proper Christian faith nor with justification. Wesley explained in his journal:

> I then met the society [at Redruth], and explained at large the rise and nature of Methodism; and still aver, I have never read or heard of, either in ancient or modern history, any other church which builds on so broad a foundation as the Methodists do; which requires of its members no conformity either in opinions or modes of worship, but barely this one thing, to fear God, and work righteousness.[72]

In this setting, then, though "fearing God and working righteousness" marks a *degree* of acceptance, it does not correspond to redemption, properly speaking, since such faith is not characterized by initially sanctifying (regenerating) grace, that grace which makes *holy*, but only by prevenient grace. Otherwise Wesley would have required both justification and the new birth (regenerating, initially sanctifying grace) in order to join a Methodist society in the first place! Again, the grace entailed in "fearing God and working righteousness" is a measure of grace, to be sure, and Wesley certainly did not want to discourage these believers—as he once had mistakenly done—who were clearly on the path of redemption; hence his positive evaluation and encouraging words.

But Wesley also employed the phrase "fear God and worketh righteousness" in a second sense, in a narrow way, which *includes* both justification and the new birth (and corresponds to the exceptions or exempt cases noted earlier) and is thereby linked with the motif of real Christianity itself. For example, in the sermon "On Divine Providence," Wesley noted, "Within the third, the innermost circle, are contained only the real Christians, those that worship God, not in form only, but in spirit and in truth. Herein are comprised all that love God, or at least truly fear God and work righteousness."[73]

What Lord Acton did in the nineteenth century—and what is still done today—was to confuse these senses, to take the attributes of the one (narrow sense) and apply them to the other (broad sense) with the result that it looked like Wesley had taught that one could become *holy* by being sincere or by the ministrations of prevenient grace rather than by initially *sanctifying* (regenerating) grace. In other words, knowing that Wesley did indeed identify the faith of one who "fears God and works righteousness" with justification and the new birth in this second, more restricted, sense, as noted, Acton mistakenly reasoned that *every* use of this phrase entailed justifying and regenerating grace for Wesley, that is, redemption properly speaking. The Cambridge professor was therefore quite puzzled when he discerned that Wesley often employed the phrase in a very general way, even with respect to non-Christians.

Again, mixing these senses, Acton could only conclude that Wesley was teaching that men and women were saved, properly speaking, by nothing more than expressing sincerity or by doing the best that they were able in terms of prevenient grace. If this were what Wesley had actually meant by the phrase "fear God and work righteousness," then the British historian and philosopher's judgment would have been accurate. Again, if it were true, then Wesley not only would have separated from the Anglican Church in the year 1767, as Acton claimed, but he would also have thoroughly undermined the standard he had championed for the proper Christian faith throughout much of his life. In effect, Wesley would have repudiated the main purpose for the rise of Methodism in the first place, that is, spreading scriptural *holiness* across the land. Wesley, of course, had done no such thing. Instead, he blended pastoral consideration for those who were responding to the prevenient grace of God with a steady determination to maintain the standard of what it meant to be a Christian, properly speaking—someone who had, through the initially sanctifying (regenerating) grace of God, become *holy*. Like the driver who has taken the wrong fork in the road, Acton thought that Wesley's theology had gone down a path that it had, in fact, never traveled.

Fearing God
and Honoring the King

Throughout much of the first half of the eighteenth century, Britain's economy was still focused on the manual production of products, many of which were agricultural. In a real sense, it was a nation of merchants and trade, with London as its economic center. However, toward the end of the century, with many scientific advances in place, in particular James Watt's steam engine in 1775, Britain began the process that has been called an "industrial revolution." Labor was slowly transferred from manually produced goods to manufactured ones, technical efficiency rose dramatically due to the increased use of machines, and tasks became increasingly routine and specialized with the result that significantly more goods were produced than ever before. Since the manufacturing process required large, central locations, this inevitably fostered urbanization. Moreover, since industrialization also demanded large investments of capital, in its wake new class distinctions arose, as well as the urban poor.

As a result of his travels throughout Britain, Wesley was well acquainted with some of the more regrettable consequences of this revolution. To ameliorate the plight of the poor, to effect a measure of social justice, Wesley took a number of steps: First of all, he adeptly used the Methodist societies which were sprinkled throughout the land as a means of aiding those in greatest need. Class meetings, for example, raised money, gathered foodstuffs, fuel, clothing, and medicine, and distributed them among the Methodist indigent. Second, as early as 1746, Wesley had provided medical care for the downtrodden of the societies and later on published the self-help manual *Primitive Physic,* a volume which, though well-intentioned, offered "folk remedies" that were hardly effective. Third, Wesley established a loan fund as well as a system for finding jobs for those who were members of a Methodist class meeting. By 1767, as Marquardt points out, "the loan fund was increased to 120 pounds, and the number of borrowers multiplied."[1] That same year Wesley "made a push for the lending-stock," as he put it, "speaking more strongly than ever [he] had done before."[2]

During the 1770s, Wesley once again inveighed against the dangers of wealth by reminding the Methodists of their obligation to forsake their "luxuries" in order to provide the necessities of life for their neighbors. Earlier, in his sermon "The Use of Money," Wesley had stressed the duty of not only gaining and saving, but also of giving all one could. However, if the obligation of giving all one could were neglected, one would run the risk of corruption and loss of faith precisely through the accumulation of wealth. "The dangers of prosperity are great; and you seem to be aware of them," Wesley counseled Dr. Wrangel in January 1770. "If poverty contracts and depresses the mind, riches sap its fortitude, destroy its vigor, and nourish its caprices."[3] These views help to explain Wesley's apparent preoccupation with such mundane matters as dress. Behind such concern, however, was not a dour, censorious spirit but one that saw any sort of extravagance or self-indulgence, such as the wearing of fine clothes, as "robbery" of the poor. Simply put, the money could have been more wisely spent.

Though Wesley had reflected on the issues of poverty and wealth throughout his ministry, it really was not until the 1770s that he began to grapple in a serious way with some of the underlying, systemic causes of poverty. For example, in 1773, in "Thoughts on the Present Scarcity of Provisions," he attempted to determine why thousands of people were still starving in Britain, why unemployment remained a problem, and why food and land were so costly. With a logic, however, more suited to a mercantile age than to a capitalist one, Wesley laid the lion's share of the remaining economic malaise on "distilling, taxes, and luxury," three of his more enduring concerns.[4]

During the eighteenth century, Britain had hoped to improve its economic situation through its foreign investments. In this plan, the American colonies would provide the mother country with raw materials as well as with a sizable income through the levying of taxes. Many of the Americans, however, chafed under the arrangement, especially during the 1770s, and the popular cry soon became "taxation without representation is tyranny." At first, Wesley was actually sympathetic to the colonial cause and believed that his own country had acted imprudently on occasion. By the middle of the decade, however, he had changed his mind, as evidenced by his remarks to Lord North on June 15, 1775:

> I do not intend to enter upon the question of whether the Americans are in the right or in the wrong. Here all my prejudices are against the Americans; for I am an High Churchman, the son of an High Churchman, bred up from my childhood in the highest notions of passive obedience and non-resistance.[5]

These comments to North are intriguing in the sense that Wesley had connected the temporal and spiritual realms, that is, the political order with an ecclesiastical one. Such a link was standard fare for many of England's eighteenth-century Tories, having been schooled on such notions since the Anglican Reformation. "There is the closest connexion . . . between my religious and my political conduct," Wesley wrote in 1777, "the selfsame authority enjoining me to 'fear God' and to 'honour the King.'"[6] That Wesley had actually drunk deeply from the wells of this long-standing tradition is also evidenced by his tying together his doctrine of Christian perfection with obedience to King George, the Hanoverian monarch. "Those who are the avowed enemies of Christian Perfection," Wesley observed, "are in general the warmest enemies of King George and of all that are in authority under him."[7]

During this time of colonial unrest, Wesley read Samuel Johnson's *Taxation No Tyranny* and was so deeply impressed by its argument that he reproduced much of it, without proper attribution, in his own "Calm Address to Our American Colonies." In this treatise, Wesley reminded the American colonists that they were no longer in the state of nature but had "sunk down" into colonists, and were governed by a charter.[8] As a result, England had the right to tax the colonists for the benefit of the whole empire. "You are the descendants of men," Wesley reasoned, "who either had no votes, or resigned them by emigration. You have therefore exactly what your ancestors left you; not a vote in making laws, nor in choosing legislators; but the happiness of being protected by laws, and the duty of obeying them."[9] For Wesley, at least, the political direction was clear, and he intended to inform the colonists, both Methodist and non-Methodist alike, of their rightful duties as British subjects.

Interestingly, Methodism in the American colonies during the early 1770s was largely a lay movement. For instance, around 1760 Robert Strawbridge, an immigrant farmer, had organized meetings in both Maryland and Virginia. Farther north, Philip Embury and his cousin, Barbara Heck, began a successful lay ministry in New York in 1766, and a year later Captain Thomas Webb (whose highest military rank was actually that of lieutenant) labored in Philadelphia. To aid these plantings of American Methodism, Wesley sent two of his more gifted lay preachers to the colonies in 1769, Richard Boardman and Joseph Pilmore. Two years later, Francis Asbury, who was to become the "Father of American Methodism," as well as Richard Wright joined their numbers.

Given the different cultural and political environment of the American colonies, Wesley's counsel was not always appreciated, even by some of the American Methodists. Indeed, believing in the superiority of constitutional monarchies, Wesley actually looked with disfavor on republican governments, writing in 1775, "No governments under heaven are so despotic as the republican; no subjects are governed in so arbitrary a manner as those of a commonwealth."[10] The political thought which informed such judgments was made explicit a year later in the treatise, "Some Observations on Liberty." Here Wesley maintained that the origin of power is not from the people (as the American colonists had supposed) but from God. "The greater share the people have in Government," Wesley argued, "the less liberty, either civil or religious, does the nation in general enjoy."[11] Francis Asbury, deeply committed to American democracy, found such views disappointing, and they naturally posed problems for the American Methodists from time to time, problems that Congregationalists and Presbyterians hardly suffered at all.

It is quite ironic that shortly before Wesley began discoursing on justice on a grand scale, that is, on the political level in terms of both Britain and her American colonies, his personal life was deeply troubled. His wife, Mary, pained by the ongoing inattention, left Wesley once again in September 1774. A month before Mary left, Wesley had imprudently decided to draft a letter and rehash nearly all the faults of his wife from the time of their wedding some twenty-three years earlier to the present. Naturally, the incidents surrounding Sarah Ryan were recounted in some detail as was Mary's practice of opening her husband's correspondence. Perhaps Wesley reopened these old wounds because he wanted to give added force to the letter's conclusion that a wife should be utterly humble, insignificant, and governed by her husband—the only solution to his marital discord that this erring husband was apparently willing to recognize. As in the past, Wesley cautioned his wife,

> Do not any longer contend for mastery, for power, money, or praise. Be content to be a private, insignificant person, known and loved by God and me. Attempt no more to abridge me of the liberty which I claim by the laws of God and man. Leave *me* to be governed by God and my own conscience. Then shall I govern *you* with gentle sway.[12]

This was hardly a prescription for reconciliation. Such appeals had not worked in the past; they would not work now or in the future.

Though the couple was separated in 1774, an arrangement apparently agreeable to both parties, this by no means put an end to the relationship. Indeed, John and Mary Wesley continued to correspond with each other at least until October 1778. One issue that surfaced in this late correspondence was Mary's poor judgment in relating some of her husband's incautious remarks to his opponents, namely, the Calvinistic Methodists—a group estranged from Wesley earlier in the decade. And though this particular incident of informing Wesley's detractors of his faults actually began in 1775, it does not appear in the extant correspondence until 1777, at which time Wesley complained,

> Likewise you have spoken all manner of evil against me, particularly to my enemies and the enemies of the cause I live to support. Hereby many bad men have triumphed and been confirmed in their evil ways; . . . a sword has been put into the hands of the enemies of God, and the children of God have been armed against one another.[13]

In past separations, when Mary had fled the Wesley home, John was willing to allow her to return whenever she pleased and without stipulation, but this was no longer the case. Indeed, in the same letter in which Wesley criticized his wife's actions, he also laid down three conditions which had to be met before she could return: (1) restore his papers; (2) promise to take no more; (3) retract what she had said against him.[14] Mary had left easily in the past; she could no longer easily return. Forgiveness was now laden with conditions.

With the deterioration of the relationship, the very last letter Wesley wrote to his wife was by no means conciliatory. Wesley saw too clearly the injustices done to him to be well aware of his wife's own justified grievances. Sadly, the letter is composed of little more than a repetition of past charges, and it concludes with an even larger condition for return: "If you were to live a thousand years," Wesley declared to his wife, "you could not undo the mischief that you have done. And till you have done all you can towards it, I bid you farewell."[15] Conditions or not, Mary was not about to return. The years of travel, relative neglect, and life with an authoritarian, and at times self-righteous, husband had taken their toll.

When Mary Wesley died a few years later on October 8, 1781, John was not immediately informed; consequently, he did not attend her funeral. But one suspects that even if Wesley had been aware of the time and place of the service, he would not have attended—a suspicion strengthened by Telford's observation that Mary's death left "no ripple on the correspondence."[16] The last breach had been that wide.

As if the difficult breakup of Wesley's marriage during the 1770s weren't enough, his relationship with the Calvinist Methodists soon deteriorated. Like his marriage, the relationship with the Calvinists was complicated, leaving room for much misunderstanding, and it was worsened by Wesley's own actions. For instance, wanting to spark a conversation with the Calvinists over some key theological issues, Wesley crudely summarized what he took to be the teachings of August Toplady, curate at Broad Hembury and author of the hymn "Rock of Ages." Not content with this, Wesley then had the audacity to affix Toplady's initials, without his permission, to the oddly drawn document:

One in twenty (suppose) of mankind are elected; nineteen in twenty are reprobated. The elect shall be saved, do what they will; the reprobate shall be damned, do what they can. Reader, believe this, or be damned. Witness my hand, A——T——.[17]

Naturally, Toplady was incensed and wanted to engage his critic in dialogue, but Wesley simply refused. "Mr. Augustus Toplady I know well," Wesley opined, "But I do not fight with chimney-sweepers. He is too dirty a writer for me to meddle with. I should only foul my fingers."[18]

Wesley's relationship with the Calvinists had taken a turn for the worse when George Whitefield, the gifted orator and Calvinist leader, died at Newburyport, Massachusetts, on his seventh preaching tour of America. The trustees of the Tabernacle at Greenwich in England invited Wesley to preach the funeral sermon there on November 23, 1770. Accepting this opportunity to praise his colleague in ministry, and perhaps also to put a good face on what had been at times a difficult relationship, Wesley chose as his text Numbers 23:10, "Let me die the death of the righteous, and let my last end be like his." In the third part of his sermon, Wesley underscored the fundamental doctrines that Whitefield had proclaimed, namely, justification by faith and the new birth, but never once mentioned the "eternal covenant" or absolute predestination. This omission, naturally, roiled Whitefield's Calvinist friends, and thus the seeds were planted for the fierce controversy that was soon to come.

Even before Whitefield's death, at the Methodist Conference in August 1770 Wesley and his preachers concluded that they had leaned too much toward Calvinism. This observation had been made in 1744, but now it was offered with more force and with even less guarded language in eight propositions. Lady Huntingdon, who was the patron of many of the Calvinist Methodists, and who had also founded a college at Trevecca, referred to the Minutes of the Conference as "popery unmasked."[19] Accordingly, in January 1771 she dismissed Joseph Benson from Trevecca for what amounted to adherence to Wesley's "popish" views. The saintly John Fletcher, confidant of Wesley's and president of the college, resigned in support of Benson, his protégé.

Somewhat surprised by the energy of the Calvinist reaction, in particular the criticism he received in the first half of 1771 at the hands of William Romaine in the *Gospel Magazine,* Wesley reviewed the whole affair in a letter to Mary Bishop, concluding with respect to the "infamous" eight propositions, "The more I consider them, the more I like them, the more fully I am convinced, not only that they are true, agreeable both to Scripture and to sound experience, but that they contain truths of the deepest importance."[20] Moreover, writing to John Fletcher on March 22, 1771, Wesley affirmed that the blood and righteousness of Christ are the sole meritorious cause of our salvation and then inquired, "Who is there in England that has asserted these things more strongly than I have done?"[21]

Walter Shirley, the cousin of Selina Lady Huntingdon, however, was not convinced. Sensing that the Conference Minutes of 1770 contained a "dreadful heresy," Shirley issued a "circular letter" which proposed that a rival conference be held in August 1771, at the same time as Wesley's upcoming meeting in Bristol. In addition, the letter recommended that the rival conference go as a body to Wesley's assembly and insist on a formal recantation of the Minutes of the previous year. The wide circulation of this letter, the language of which in several places was unguarded, polarized the theological parties for a time. Lady Glenorchy, for example, dismissed Wesley's preachers from her chapel shortly after its publication. The letter also created significant interest in the 1771 Conference, and Wesley noted quite wryly in his journal that "we had more preachers than usual at the Conference in consequence of Mr. Shirley's circular letter."[22]

As promised, on August 8, 1771, Shirley and nine or ten others attended the conference at Bristol. After much discussion, Wesley concluded that "they were satisfied that we were not so dreadful heretics as they imagined, but were tolerably sound in the faith."[23] In an irenic move, Wesley and his preachers issued a clarifying statement of the earlier minutes. The statement is worth quoting at length:

> Whereas the doctrinal points in the Minutes of a Conference held in London, August 7th, 1770, have been understood to favour justification by works—now, we, the Rev. John Wesley and others assembled in Conference, do declare that we had no such meaning, and

that we abhor the doctrine of justification by works as a most perilous and abominable doctrine. And as the said Minutes are not sufficiently guarded in the way they are expressed, we hereby solemnly declare, in the sight of God, that we have no trust or confidence but in the alone merits of our Lord and Saviour, Jesus Christ, for justification or salvation, either in life, death or the day of judgment. And though no one is a *real* Christian believer (and consequently cannot be saved) who doth not good works when there is time and opportunity, yet our works have no part in meriting or purchasing our justification, from first to last, either in whole or in part.[24]

Such a declaration quelled the flames of controversy at least for a time, and a letter, supposedly in Shirley's own writing, acknowledged that he had been too hasty in his judgment of Wesley's sentiments.[25]

But all was not well. No sooner had the ink fully dried on Wesley's declaration than he sent off John Fletcher's *Vindication* of the Minutes of 1770 for publication, notwithstanding Walter Shirley's earnest request not to do so. Fletcher, who at times was referred to as Wesley's "Vindicator," had been associated with the father of Methodism for several years. Born in Switzerland of a distinguished family, Fletcher refused to subscribe to some of the teachings of Calvinism, and he thus declined Swiss ordination as a young man. Emigrating to England in 1752, Fletcher served as a capable tutor and was soon attracted by the piety and earnestness of the Methodists. On March 6, 1757, after consultation with Wesley, Fletcher was ordained deacon in the Church of England and a priest the following Sunday. A man not only of deep piety, Fletcher also possessed great intellectual skills—skills that Wesley clearly wanted to utilize given his current predicament. In fact, so confident was Wesley in Fletcher's ability, in his carefully reasoned arguments, that he wrote to the Countess of Huntingdon less than a week after the 1771 Conference:

> "The principles established in the *Minutes*" I apprehend to be no way contrary to this, or to that faith, that consistent plan of doctrine, which was once delivered to the saints. I believe, whoever calmly considers Mr. Fletcher's Letters will be convinced of this. I fear, therefore, "zeal against those principles" is no less than zeal against the truth and against the honour of our Lord. "The preservation of

His honour appears so sacred" to *me,* and has done for above these forty years.[26]

And then in what looked like a retraction of his earlier, conciliatory declaration, Wesley was now so emboldened by his colleague's work as to declare to the Countess, "But till Mr. Fletcher's printed letters are answered, I must think everything spoke against those *Minutes* is totally destructive of His honour, and a palpable affront to Him both as our Prophet and Priest, but more especially as King of His people."[27]

Encouraged by the reception of his *Vindication* and also by Wesley, John Fletcher published his first and second *Checks to Antinomianism* the following month. Wesley especially liked the title of these apologetic works since he believed that Calvinism could easily become "a deadly enemy to all Christian tempers."[28] Not surprisingly, the publication of the *Checks* brought the controversy to a new level of intensity. Rowland Hill, who preached for the Countess in her chapels, entered the fray in the middle of 1772 with his *Friendly Remarks upon Fletcher's Checks.* It was Fletcher's second *Check* which had convinced Hill that he could no longer remain silent. And a few years later, in 1777, Hill published his *Imposture Detected,* a work with an acerbic tone. Of this piece, Wesley related, "I read the truly wonderful performance of Mr. Rowland Hill. I stood amazed! Compared to him Mr. Toplady himself is a very civil, fair-spoken gentleman."[29]

Richard Hill, the brother of Rowland, picked up his pen in opposition after the publication of Fletcher's *Third Check to Antinomianism.* One of his more important works was "Review of all the Doctrines Taught by Mr. John Wesley." Irked, Wesley countered with "Some Remarks on Mr. Hill's 'Review of all the Doctrines Taught by Mr. John Wesley'" (September 1772), in which he pointed out the logical inconsistencies in Hill's own argument, its erroneous presuppositions and assumptions, as well as Hill's annoying habit of quoting the language of *A Christian Library* as if it were Wesley's own. In his *Finishing Stroke,* published the following year, Hill turned his attention not so much toward Wesley as toward Fletcher and accused him of caricaturing the Calvinist position. Fletcher's reply in this particular instance as well as his general comportment throughout the entire controversy convinced Wesley that he had finally found a suitable successor, a champion even, to lead the Methodists after he was gone. "But has God provided one so qualified? Who is he? Thou art the man!" Wesley declared to Fletcher in January 1773. But such an honor was not to be, for John Fletcher, who had suffered ill health from time to time, not only declined the offer but also died about six years prior to John Wesley.

What was it about the Conference Minutes of 1770 that had so disturbed the Calvinists? For one thing, this theological document was characterized by an imperative mood that employed such language as "work, labor, and obedience," which some took to undermine the doctrine of justification by faith alone. For example, in the first thesis the Conference concluded that "we ought steadily to assert upon his [Christ's] authority, that if a man is not faithful in the unrighteous mammon, God will not give him the true riches." The next theological proposition developed this imperative mood even further and indicated, once again, in what way the Methodists had leaned too much toward Calvinism:

> With regard to "working for life," which our Lord expressly commands us to do. "Labour," literally, *"work,* for the meat that endureth to everlasting life." And in fact, every believer, till he comes to glory, works *for* as well as *from* life.

Beyond this, the third thesis affirmed that those who are *now* accepted of God believe in Christ "with a loving, *obedient* heart."[30]

Such emphases led the Calvinists to conclude that Wesley was, in effect, teaching salvation by works. Wesley, however, refuted this criticism in a letter to several preachers and friends, drafted on July 10, 1771, by making a distinction between *gaining* the favor of God and *being* in that favor:

> "Who of us is *now* accepted of God?" (I mean, who is now in His favour? The question does not refer to the *gaining* the favour of God, but the *being* therein, at any given point of time.) "He that now believes in Christ with a loving and obedient heart."[31]

In fairness to the Calvinist party, the Countess of Huntingdon and Walter Shirley among them, it must be noted that Wesley's precise distinction did not clear up all of the problems, especially when the 1770 Conference had gone on to affirm that those who do not know Christ are *accepted* of God and remain in that acceptance by "fearing God and working righteousness." Such language, without qualification, was unguarded and no doubt led to Wesley's earlier, conciliatory tone. Indeed, this phrasing could easily lead to the conclusion that all that was required for redemption for those who did not know Christ was sincerity or simply doing the best that they were able in response to *prevenient* grace. If that were the case, then the Calvinists would indeed have had substantial grounds for complaint.

But as it was, the Calvinists had missed key theological distinctions—and Wesley didn't help them much at the time—which were the required background for a proper interpretation of the statement "fearing God and working righteousness." As we saw in chapter 7, for Wesley, there were *degrees* of acceptance (due to prevenient grace), but not all degrees *necessarily* entailed justifying, regenerating faith, that distinct faith which delivers from both the guilt and power of sin—a faith, in other words, that both receives forgiveness and makes one initially *holy*. For example, at times Wesley employed the phrase "feareth God and worketh righteousness," to refer in a narrow sense to the "exceptions" or "exempt" cases, who though justified and born of God, yet lacked assurance. Accordingly, Wesley wrote to Ann Bolton on August 12, 1770, reasoning,

> "He that feareth God," says the Apostle, "and worketh righteousness," though but in a low *degree*, is accepted of Him; more especially when such an one trusts not in his own righteousness but in the atoning blood. I cannot doubt at all but this is your case; though you have not that joy in the Holy Ghost to which you are called, because your faith is weak and only as a grain of mustard seed.[32]

But Wesley also employed the phrase "fearing God and working righteousness" in a broad sense, one that entailed neither being a child of God nor redemption, properly speaking. Such usage pertained not only to those who "knew not Christ" but also to those who had indeed heard the gospel but who were not yet the children of God, renewed in holiness. On August 29, 1777, Wesley wrote to Alexander Knox and elaborated:

You should read Mr. Fletcher's *Essay on Truth*. He has there put it beyond all doubt that there is a medium between a child of God and a child of the devil—namely, a servant of God. This is *your* state. You are not yet a son, but you are a servant; and you are waiting for the Spirit of adoption, which will cry in your heart, "Abba, Father." You have "received the Spirit of grace," and *in a measure* work righteousness.[33]

Without understanding these different senses and also because they were not privy to the intricacies of Wesley's doctrine of prevenient grace, the Calvinists of 1770 could only conclude, just as Lord Acton did much later, that not only was Wesley teaching salvation by works, but also that he had undermined the doctrine of justification by faith by allowing his theology to devolve into moralism, self-effort, and pious platitudes. The reality, however, was quite different. A careful examination of Wesley's sermon "The Scripture Way of Salvation," would perhaps have convinced the Calvinists that in Wesley's estimation works could never justify, only grace could justify. Unfortunately, much was lost in the heat of the polemics.

To be sure, the energetic criticism of the Calvinist controversy flowed in both directions. The Minutes of 1770 had contained an explicit critique of Calvinism. As in 1739 with the publication of the sermon "Free Grace," as in 1740 before the Fetter Lane Society, and as in 1744 before Oxford University, Wesley had hoped to spark a debate with the publication of the Minutes of 1770 concerning theological matters he deemed particularly important. Clearly, both Wesley and Fletcher had come to believe that Calvinism could foster antinomianism; that is, Reformed theological teachings could undermine the importance of being *holy*. "I am afraid Lady Huntingdon's preachers will do little good wherever they go," Wesley wrote to Mrs. Woodhouse in 1773. "They are wholly swallowed up in that detestable doctrine of predestination, and can talk of nothing else."[34] A year later Wesley wrote to Fletcher that after justification God is pleased or displeased with believers according to the actual tempers of their hearts and according to their works. "I see more and more clearly," he observed, "that 'there is a great gulf fixed' between us and all those who, by denying this, sap the very foundation both of inward and outward holiness."[35] And Wesley's tone became even more serious when in 1777 he cautioned Francis Wolfe, "O beware of Calvinism and everything that has the least tendency thereto. Let a burnt child dread the fire!"[36]

One of the more important issues at the heart of the Calvinist controversy, at least from Wesley's perspective, was the whole question of the actualization or realization of grace in holy tempers—tempers integral to Wesley's understanding of what it means to be a real, scriptural Christian. Wesley believed that the very substance of Christianity was being redefined or explained away in the wake of Calvinist distinctives, the doctrines of the decrees as well as the perseverance of the saints chief among them. It is, therefore, not surprising that during the 1770s, as well as in the following decade, Wesley wrote more on the theme of real Christianity than at any other time in his career. Given the challenge of antinomianism, Wesley was decidedly intent on defining Christianity, properly speaking, as entailing nothing less than the realization of that grace which makes one *holy*.

During this period, then, Wesley underscored the truth that real Christians are those whose inward (and outward) lives have been transformed by the bountiful regenerating grace of God. "Unless they have new senses, ideas, passions, [and] tempers," Wesley counseled, "they are no Christians."[37] Indeed, when Wesley was in Ireland during 1773, while the Calvinist controversy was still raging, he asked himself the question concerning the citizens of Galway, among whom were twenty thousand Catholics and five hundred Protestants, "But which of them are Christians? Have the mind that was in Christ and walk as he walked?"[38]—a question which amply suggests his yet lofty standards for being a Christian. Of his own people, the "English Christians in general," he wryly noted in 1776 that they "know no more of Christian salvation [and hence of inward transformation] than Mahometans or heathens."[39] And two years later, in a letter to Mary Bishop, Wesley made abundantly clear—probably thinking of the work of Calvinist "gospel" preachers—what was at the heart of salvation:

> Let but a pert, self-sufficient animal, that has neither sense nor grace, bawl out something about Christ and His blood or justification by faith, and his hearers cry out, "What a fine gospel sermon!"

Surely the Methodists have not so learnt Christ. We know no gospel without salvation from sin.[40]

One of the great attractions of Calvinist theology, of course, was the comfort it could bring believers in knowing that their redemption was utterly in the hands of God through the inscrutable decrees. As such, the elect would not, indeed, could not be lost. In a real sense, Wesley's doctrine of Christian assurance—an assurance which develops as one grows in grace and becomes *increasingly* holy—was an answer, in part, to the comfort that Calvinist notions of predestination and election could afford. By 1771, for example, Wesley had distinguished full assurance, which excludes doubt and fear, from initial assurance which does not; he had come to a greater appreciation of the faith of a servant and its degree of acceptance; and he had realized that in exceptional cases one may even be justified and yet lack assurance, either due to ignorance of the gospel promises or due to bodily disorder. Nevertheless, the theme Wesley chose to develop during this late period of his life, in the midst of the Calvinist controversy, was none other than a strong identification of assurance with the proper (real) Christian faith. In his sermon "On the Trinity" (1775), he declared:

> But I know not how *anyone* can be a Christian believer till "he hath" (as St. John speaks) "the witness in himself"; till "the Spirit of God witnesses with his spirit that he is a child of God"—that is, in effect, till God the Holy Ghost witnesses that God the Father has accepted him through the merits of God the Son.[41]

Here there would be no consolation from decrees nor from doctrinal teaching and the like. Instead, assurance would be given to the soul *directly* by the presence of the Spirit who makes one holy.

In 1778, Wesley continued his critique of Calvinism by publishing the first edition of the *Arminian Magazine,* a journal that consisted of "Extracts and Original Treaties on Universal Redemption." As Wesley's answer to the Calvinist *Gospel Magazine,* the *Arminian Magazine* brought forth "some of the most remarkable tracts on the universal love of God and on His willingness to save all men from all sin."[42] A few years earlier, Wesley had expressed similar sentiments when he wrote to Francis Wolfe,

"Nothing will so effectually stop the plague of Calvinism as the preaching salvation from all sin and exhorting all to expect it now by naked faith."[43]

By the end of the decade, the Calvinist controversy had basically run its course, not because the two parties had come to some sort of agreement—indeed they were as far apart as ever—but because many involved were simply tired of the polemics. In the meantime, Wesley's ministry in London was prospering, and so he turned his attention to other matters, including plans for replacing the Foundery, a building that had served the Methodists so well in the past. The new structure, which became known variously as "Wesley's Chapel," the "New Chapel," or simply "City Road Chapel," was built not far from the old Foundery, directly across from Bunhill Fields. The foundation stone for the Chapel was laid, with some celebration, on April 21, 1777, and the building was formally opened by Wesley on November 1, 1778. Of its design, Wesley noted in his journal, "It is perfectly neat, but not fine"[44]—architecture, in other words, well suited to the Methodists.

It is fitting that Wesley continually paid attention to the institutional needs of Methodism in order to ensure that its genius, especially its emphasis on holy love, would be passed from generation to generation. This task became increasingly important toward the end of the decade and into the next, simply because Wesley would soon take action which, despite his own protests to the contrary, would move Methodism beyond the ecclesiastical perimeters of the Church of England. What Charles Wesley had feared all along was about to take place.

9

Building a Legacy

Recognizing that the work of Methodism in America was in great need of suitable laborers, Wesley entreated Dr. Lowth, the Bishop of London, to that end in August 1780. "There are three ministers in that country already," the bishop exclaimed. "True, my Lord," Wesley replied, "but what are three to watch over all the souls in that extensive country?"[1] Realizing that his powers of persuasion had failed, Wesley became increasingly critical of the bishop's ordination practices. Wesley's words are worth quoting at length because they not only express his frustration with respect to furthering the work of God in America, but they also give evidence of his conception of vital gospel ministry:

> I have heard that your Lordship is unfashionably diligent in examining the candidates for Holy Orders—yea, that your Lordship is generally at the pains of examining them *yourself*. Examining them! In what respects? Why, whether they understand a little *Latin* and *Greek* and can answer a few trite questions in the science of divinity! Alas, how little does this avail! Does your Lordship examine whether they serve *Christ* or *Belial*? whether they love God or the world? whether they ever had any serious thoughts about heaven or hell? whether they have any real desire to save their own souls or the souls of others? If not, what have they to do with Holy Orders? and what will become of the souls committed to their care?[2]

In his reply, Wesley by no means deprecated the importance of learning for vital ministry, as his earlier treatise on this topic, *An Address to the Clergy* (1756), clearly demonstrated. Rather, he underscored the importance *also* of the knowledge of practical divinity, specifically the wisdom and grace required in saving souls. "My Lord, I do by no means despise learning," Wesley noted. "I know the value of it too well. But what is this, particularly in a Christian minister, compared to piety? What is it in a man that has no religion? 'As a jewel in a swine's snout.'" Expressing his frustration and in a way that was sure to irritate the bishop, Wesley added, "Your Lordship did see good to ordain and send into America other persons who knew something of Greek and Latin, but who knew no more of saving souls than of catching whales."[3]

But perhaps Wesley's lively conversation with the Bishop of London was nearly moot by this time for the political and religious situation in America was changing rapidly. In 1780 the British army was soundly defeated at King's Mountain, North Carolina. The following year, the British troops, nearly exhausted, were again defeated in battles at Cowpens and Eutaw, North Carolina. Finally, all land operations on American soil ceased with the British capitulation at Yorktown, at which point Charleston and Savannah were soon evacuated. Thus, the very places where the Wesleys had begun their ministry in America during the 1730s now experienced the British retreat.

Since in Wesley's mind the Church of England was in some sense tied to the temporal order, that is, to the British nation and its colonies, any change in that order would necessitate a change in the religious one as well. Accordingly, reflecting on the American situation in 1784, Wesley reasoned in his treatise *To Our Brethren in America*, "As our American brethren are now totally disentangled both from the State and from the English hierarchy, we dare not entangle them again either with the one or the other. They are now at full liberty simply to follow the Scriptures and the Primitive Church."[4]

Emboldened by his earlier readings of Lord Peter King and Edward Stillingfleet, as noted in chapter 7, and encouraged by the changed American political situation, Wesley was determined to act decisively in the face of both the great need in America and the ongoing indifference on the part of the Anglican hierarchy. Exercising the role of bishop at the 1784 Conference, Wesley set apart Thomas Coke as superintendent by the imposition of hands and by prayer. Wesley's diary referred to this event using the word "ordained." His journal, however, stated that Dr. Coke was "appointed," and the actual certificate given to the new superintendent employed the words "set apart." Once in America, Thomas Coke, who brought Wesley's *Sunday Service* with him, had instructions to consecrate Francis Asbury as General Superintendent, a ceremony which took place at the founding Christmas Conference of 1784. Beyond this, Wesley himself ordained Richard Whatcoat and Thomas Vasey as elders in order to foster the work of the Methodists in America.

Wesley justified such irregular actions—at least by Anglican standards—by noting that "the case is widely different between England and America. Here, therefore, my scruples are at an end."[5] And in a letter to Barnabas Thomas in March 1785, Wesley made his case along the following lines: "I am now as firmly attached to the Church of England as I ever was since you knew me. But meantime I know myself to be as real a Christian bishop as the Archbishop of Canterbury."[6] Charles Wesley, however, was not convinced. Indeed, the ordinations for America had caused a ripple in the relationship, which John quickly sought to repair. After posting several letters which insisted that he had not separated from the Church of England by his recent actions, Wesley finally came to realize that the rift between him and his brother Charles was not to be so easily managed: "I see no use of you and me disputing together; for neither of us is likely to convince the other. You say I separate from the Church; I say I do not. Then let it stand."[7]

Though Wesley appeared to be at the peak of his power over the American Methodists with his ordinations of 1784, that power, ironically, soon began to dissipate and was eventually shared by the very American leaders Wesley had appointed. For example, in September 1786, Wesley stated that the American Methodists should meet in a General Conference at Baltimore on May 1, 1787. In addition, he desired that Mr. Richard Whatcoat be appointed Superintendent to assist Francis Asbury. To Wesley's considerable dismay, both counsels were quietly put aside. Indeed, relations between Wesley and the American church in general and Francis Asbury in particular became so difficult at times that in September 1788 Wesley felt compelled to remind Asbury, "There is, indeed, a wide difference between the relation wherein you stand to the Americans and the relation wherein I stand to all the American

Methodists: I am under God the father of the whole family." And Wesley soon became angry when he learned that Asbury, not content with the title of superintendent, was now being referred to by his American colleagues as "bishop." Wesley cautioned Asbury (and Thomas Coke):

> I study to be little: you study to be great. I creep: you strut along. I found a school: you a college! nay, and call it after your own names! O beware, do not seek to be something! Let me be nothing, and "Christ be all in all." ... How can you, how dare you suffer yourself to be called Bishop? I shudder, I start at the very thought! Men may call me a knave or a fool, a rascal, a scoundrel, and I am content; but they shall never by my consent call me Bishop! For my sake, for God's sake, for Christ's sake put a full end to this![8]

Despite Wesley's energetic protestations, this counsel, too, was quietly put aside. For his part, Asbury maintained that no person in Europe knew how to direct those in America, and he told George Shadford, "Mr. Wesley and I are like Caesar and Pompei: he will bear no equal, and I will have no superior."[9]

Wesley's relation to British Methodism was, of course, much different but no less complicated. As in the past, he insisted that "when the Methodists leave the Church of England, God will leave them."[10] More to the point, Wesley tied this salient issue of separation to the larger question of formal as opposed to vital religion; in other words, he linked it to his motif of real as opposed to nominal Christianity. "Of the Methodists and the Church—they *must* not leave the Church—at least, while I live," Wesley exclaimed in 1788. "If they leave it then, I expect they will gradually sink into a formal, honorable sect."[11]

To ensure that his contribution to the British evangelical revival would not be seen as a competitor to the Anglican Church, Wesley insisted during the early part of the 1780s, as he had done earlier, that Methodist preaching services were not to be held at the same time as Anglican worship. Indeed, so concerned was Wesley about this issue that he wrote several letters to this effect. And though he cautioned in 1786 that "to fix it (Methodist preaching) at the same hour is obliging them to separate, either from the Church or us," by 1789 he was beginning to make some allowances for such an overlap and he now became unwilling to call it leaving the church. To the printer of the *Dublin Chronicle,* for example, he wrote, "Could I even then deny that I had service in church hours? No; but I denied, and do deny still, that this is leaving the Church."[12]

Many of the Methodists in Britain during the 1780s, of course, attended both Methodist and Anglican services, and it was only natural therefore to compare the two. Discerning a significant difference between these settings, some Methodists complained to Wesley that Anglican worship was led at times by priests who not only did not preach the liberty of the gospel, but whose very lives also failed to give witness to the bountiful grace of God. So concerned was Wesley about fostering scriptural Christianity—as opposed to a dead, formalistic faith—that he directed those under his spiritual care even to the point of forsaking Anglican services:

> Those ministers (so called) who neither live nor preach the gospel I dare not say are sent of God. Where one of these is settled, many of the Methodists dare not attend his ministry; so, if there be no other church in that neighbourhood, they go to church no more.[13]

Such direction fell under Wesley's larger principle of what must be done by *necessity* in order to care for souls. This same principle was in play at the Methodist Conference of 1788, which not only drew the by-now-familiar distinction between doctrine and discipline but which also went on to indicate that Methodist variance with respect to the latter was in each instance due to *necessity,* due to the requirement of saving souls, the very imperative of the gospel. Accordingly, the Conference came to the following conclusions:

> (1) That, in a course of fifty years, we had neither premeditately nor willingly varied from [the Church of England] in one article either of doctrine or discipline; (2) That we were not yet conscious of varying from it in any point of doctrine; (3) That we have in a course of years, out of *necessity,* not choice, slowly and warily varied in some points of discipline, by preaching in the fields, by extemporary prayer, by employing lay preachers, by forming and regulating societies, and by holding yearly Conferences. But we did none of these things till we were convinced we could no longer omit them but at the peril of our souls.[14]

Notice, once again, that Wesley and the Conference affirmed that the Methodists had not varied from the Church of England in the least with respect to *doctrine*. What differences there were—and there were several—fell under the broad heading of *discipline*. Here, then, we find several of the Methodist distinctives such as field preaching, extemporary prayer, employing lay preachers, forming societies, and holding Conferences. And all these elements, Wesley maintained to the chagrin of some of his Anglican peers, came about not due to whim or fancy but simply due to *necessity*, to the imperative of saving souls. "Give me one hundred preachers who fear nothing but sin and desire nothing but God," Wesley had thundered a few years earlier, "and I care not a straw whether they be clergymen or laymen, such alone will shake the gates of hell and set up the kingdom of heaven on earth."[15]

Though Wesley repeatedly affirmed that he had no desire for Methodism to leave the Church of England, he was realistic enough to prepare for just such a possibility. Indeed, the earlier promulgation of the Deed of Declaration in 1784 must not be viewed simply as the way in which Wesley provided for the institutional structure of Methodism beyond his death. The Deed must also be seen as a structure which could, if necessary, provide order for Methodism independent of the mother church. Indeed, among other things, the Deed of Declaration defined the Methodist Conference for the Trust Deeds, established a connection throughout Britain, appointed a hundred preachers as the legal Conference (thereby providing the basis for future Annual Conferences), and laid down guidelines for the reception of preachers into full connection. With such a structure in place, and if several of the members of Conference were fully ordained and thereby able to administer the sacraments, the Church of England would hardly be needed. Surely, Wesley must have realized this.

The Deed of Declaration is also interesting because it reveals Wesley's tendency, on occasion, toward autocracy in that he made allowance for only one hundred of his preachers to be a part of this legal governing body. Thomas Coke was strongly opposed to this action and believed that "all preachers in full connection should be members, as had been the case for over a dozen years before 1780."[16] At the time of the Deed's composition in 1784, there were about two hundred preachers, and it made little sense that half of them, many of whom had sacrificed much for the gospel, should be dishonored by exclusion—and in such an arbitrary manner. John Hampson, Sr., for instance, who was utterly devoted to Wesley, was not among the legal hundred—to his great dismay. Such a fanciful figure was an *inevitable* prescription for bad feelings, resentment, and the spawning of many unholy tempers. And yet Wesley accepted no responsibility for this.

The following year Wesley repeated his earlier claim that though he had never exercised in *England* the power he believed God had given him (he had already done so in America) he firmly believed himself to be a "scriptural episcopos as much as any man in England or in Europe."[17] However, shortly after this pronouncement, he began to ordain ministers for Scotland. Wesley justified this action by noting that the Church of England was not the established church in that land. He then required those who were ordained for work in Scotland to abandon their orders once they crossed the border into England. As V. H. H. Green aptly points out, "If ordination meant anything at all this was indefensible. If it was valid then it must be indelible."[18]

But Wesley did not stop there. Having ordained for America and now for Scotland, in 1788 he finally crossed the Rubicon, setting apart ministers for work in England itself. Thus, Alexander Mather was ordained deacon and presbyter on August 6 and 7, respectively. Henry Moore and Thomas Rankin were ordained the following year on February 26 and 27. By the end of his career, Wesley had actually ordained more than twenty-five ministers for work in Scotland, England, America, and even for such places as Nova Scotia, Newfoundland, and the West Indies. That Wesley was not censured for such action by his own church indicates something of the lax and indulgent standards of the time. Had he been called to task, Wesley would likely have replied that the work of the gospel *necessitated* such action, that it was far better to send in laborers to the field than to watch the harvest rot on the ground.

Robert Southey, one of the more able biographers of the nineteenth century, took issue with Wesley's repeated claims of allegiance to the Church of England in the wake of his several ordinations: "He [Wesley] had been led toward a separation imperceptibly, step by step; but it is not to his honour that he affected to deprecate it to the last, while he was evidently bringing it about by the measures which he pursued."[19] Whether Wesley's actions did indeed constitute a separation from the Anglican Church is a question that no doubt will continue to be debated.

At any rate, in his later years Wesley was not only concerned with the ongoing infrastructure of both American and British Methodism, but he was also preoccupied with the vitality, the very substance, of the Methodist faith. Wesley's principal fear in this area was that Methodism would soon devolve into a dead faith, having the outward form of religion but lacking the power thereof. Such decline, he believed, would be brought about by none other than the specter of riches. Precisely due to their diligence and frugality, qualities quite valuable in themselves, the Methodists ran the risk of becoming rich, perhaps even self-satisfied. To caution against this calamity Wesley wrote two key sermons during the 1780s, one at the beginning of the decade, the other toward the end.

In his sermon "The Danger of Riches" (1780), Wesley warned those under his direction that riches (whatever is above the plain necessities or—at most—the conveniences of life) "naturally lead to some or other...foolish and hurtful desires," such as the desire of the flesh, the desire of the eyes, and the pride of life. Moreover, Wesley discerned a close connection between the accumulation of wealth, on the one hand, and the inculcation of unholy tempers in the human heart, on the other.[20] Though he did not draw an exact equation in this area, he did associate in a strong way the graces of humility, meekness, and kindness with the poor; and pride, haughtiness, and arrogance with the rich. "Oh what advantage have the poor over the rich!" Wesley remarked in 1788. "These are not wise in their own eyes, but all receive with meekness the ingrafted word which is able to save their souls."[21]

In his sermon "On Riches" (1788), Wesley tied this whole discussion of wealth and the inculcation of holy tempers in the heart to his ongoing concern for being a real Christian:

> But it would not be strange if rich men were in general void of all good dispositions, and an easy prey to all evil ones, since so few of them pay any regard to that solemn declaration of our Lord, with-

out observing which we cannot be his disciples. . . . "If any man will come after me," will be a *real Christian*, "let him deny himself, and take up his cross daily, and follow me."[22]

In denying themselves, in being among the less fortunate, earnest Christians availed themselves of the very settings which would be most conducive to spiritual growth. For Wesley, then, it was not sufficient simply to send money to the poor. Instead, one must actually visit the poor and be among them. "O how much better is it to go to the poor than to the rich," Wesley declared earlier in the decade, "and to the house of mourning, than to the house of feasting."[23]

Precisely in order to foster fellowship between the poor and those who had more of life's means, Wesley wrote an important sermon in 1786, "On Visiting the Sick." In this sermon, in a very pastoral fashion, he advised the Methodists just how to be among the sick and poor, how to bring about the amelioration of their condition:

> But it may not be amiss usually to begin with inquiring into their outward condition. You may ask whether they have the necessaries of life. Whether they have sufficient food and raiment. If the weather be cold, whether they have fuel.[24]

But after this, Wesley asserted, the visitor is to proceed to things of *greater* value. "These little labours of love," he wrote, "will pave your way to things of *greater* importance. Having shown that you have a regard for their bodies you may proceed to inquire concerning their souls."[25] He repeated this judgment, no doubt for emphasis, but this time clearly displaying what is the goal of all gospel ministry:

> While you are as eyes to the blind and feet to the lame, a husband to the widow and a father to the fatherless, see that you still keep *a higher end in view,* even the saving of souls from death, and that you labour to make all you say and do subservient *to that great end.*[26]

These value judgments are by no means peculiar to this sermon, but represent Wesley's own best thinking throughout his career.

Much earlier, in 1748, he had written concerning those engaged in ministry that "he doth good, to the uttermost of his power, even to the bodies of men. . . . How much more does he rejoice if he can do any good to the soul of any man!"[27] Two years later he continued this theme in his sermon "Upon Our Lord's Sermon on the Mount, Discourse the Thirteenth":

> Over and above all this, are you zealous of good works? Do you, as you have time, do good to all men? Do you feed the hungry and clothe the naked, and visit the fatherless and widow in their afflic-tion? Do you visit those that are sick? Relieve them that are in prison? Is any a stranger and you take him in? Friend, *come up high-er*. . . . Does he enable you to bring sinners from darkness to light, from the power of Satan unto God?[28]

For Wesley, then, a part of what it meant to love your neighbor as yourself always involved the exercise of both material gifts and spiritual talents; it entailed the employment of all those gifts and graces which would enhance the physical well-being of the poor *and* their spiritual character. Second, and perhaps more important, though the material needs of the neighbor had chronological pri-ority (in the sense that they were the very first things to be done), they clearly did not have valuational priority in Wesley's thought,[29] for their fulfillment prepared the way, to use Wesley's own words, for things of *greater importance*.

In characteristic fashion, Wesley's own life clearly matched his teachings on this important issue of poverty and wealth. Not only did he go about begging for the poor (among some of his "rich" friends), most notably in London in 1785 and in 1787, but he also died with little more than a teapot to his name—despite the large sum of money that had flowed through his hands. Where had all the money gone? Wesley quite simply distributed it among the poor of the Methodist societies and thereby helped to bring about, at least in a small way, the kingdom of God on earth.

Though Wesley was obviously quite energetic in ministry dur-ing the 1780s, this was a very difficult decade for him personally. He was shorn of two of his dearest friends and fellow laborers. In August 1785, his designated successor, John Fletcher, died and was entombed in the churchyard in Madeley where he had labored for so many years. Wesley naturally offered much praise in remembrance of him and even wrote a brief account of Fletcher's life. A few years later, in 1788, his brother Charles, who had been with John from the very beginning of the great evangelical revival, passed away into glory. Upon learning of Charles's death, Wesley remarked, "The Lord gave, and the Lord hath taken away; blessed be the name of the Lord."[30]

Before his death, Charles, holding the notion of consecrated ground dear, left instructions that he was not to be buried in the Chapel at City Road, or in the Dissenters cemetery across the way, that is, in Bunhill Fields where his mother, Susanna, had been laid to rest. Instead, he was to be interred in Marylebone churchyard in the northwest part of London. Of this request, John remarked, "Tis pity but the remains of my brother had been deposited with me. Certainly that *ground* is *holy* [the Chapel at City Road] as any in England, and it contains a large quantity of 'bonny dust.'"[31] In death, then, as in life, Charles Wesley yet distinguished himself from his elder brother.

Of his own health, Wesley had often boasted just how good it was. Indeed, the birthday pages of his journal are filled with such material. On one such occasion, late in his career, Wesley remarked, "By the blessing of God I am just the same as when I entered the twenty-eighth [year]. This hath God wrought, chiefly by my constant exercise, my rising early, and preaching morning and evening."[32] In fact, so vigorous was Wesley at the time that he decided to take an excursion to Holland—one of his few respites from his ongoing labors—in June 1783, a place to which he returned in 1786. The trip went well, by all reports, but shortly after Wesley's return to England in August 1783, he was seized with "a most impetuous flux." A grain and a half of opium was administered to him in three doses to bring about some relief. This narcotic naturally stopped the cramps that Wesley had been suffering, but it also "took away my speech, hearing and power of motion, and locked me up from head to foot, so that I lay a mere log."[33]

Wesley soon recovered from his "flux," but the observations on his sanguine health that had marked the beginning of the decade evaporated as he approached its end. In October 1789, for instance,

Wesley noted that his sight was dimmed, his strength decreased, and "I cannot easily preach above twice a day."[34] On January 1, 1790, the elderly preacher detailed how age was now taking its toll:

> I am now an old man, decayed from head to foot. My eyes are dim; my right hand shakes much; my mouth is hot and dry every morning; I have a lingering fever almost every day; my motion is weak and slow. However, blessed be God, I do not slack my labour. I can preach and write still.[35]

Though Wesley was clearly in decline, it is remarkable that he was yet preoccupied with the theme that had surfaced in his late night conversation with the porter at Christ Church so many years before, namely, the importance of being a real Christian. Such a concern had not only remained with Wesley throughout the years, in the midst of all his labors, but it also intensified as he began to count the days which remained. To be sure, the 1780s mark Wesley's greatest interest in this theme, judging from the number of times it appeared in his writings. In 1785, for example, Wesley continued to highlight the distinction between nominal and real Christians, and pointed out in his sermon "The New Creation," employing a familiar rhetoric by now, that the former "have the form of godliness without the power."[36] Clues, by the way, as to when Wesley himself determined in his own mind to be a real Christian are found in a late sermon, "In What Sense We Are to Leave the World," where he indicated, once again, the significance of the year 1725: "When it pleased God to give me a settled resolution to be not a nominal but a real Christian (being about two and twenty years of age) my acquaintance were as ignorant of God as myself."[37]

As in an earlier period, Wesley reflected back on the Oxford Methodists, but this time in a letter to Henry Brooke (1786), where he avowed that their original design was nothing less than to be "Bible Christians."[38] Moreover, the following year, in his sermon "Of Former Times," Wesley revealed that the goal of "the Holy Club" was above all to help one another to be "real Christians."[39] But perhaps the most noteworthy accent during this late interval of Wesley's life was his strong identification of real, scriptural

Christianity with the new birth and, therefore, with all the marks of the new birth such as faith, hope, and love. For example, in a pastoral letter to his nephew Samuel Wesley, who had converted to Roman Catholicism (though he later renounced this move), Wesley cautioned, "'Except a man be born again, . . . he cannot see the kingdom of heaven' except he experience that inward change of the earthly, sensual mind for the mind which was in Christ Jesus."[40] And a year later, in 1789, Wesley's strong identification of real Christianity with regeneration, with the children of God, was again unmistakable. "How great a thing it is to be a Christian," he declares in his sermon "On a Single Eye," "to be a real, inward, scriptural Christian! Conformed in heart and life to the will of God! Who is sufficient for these things? None, unless he be born of God."[41]

It was also during the decade of the 1780s—when Wesley became an octogenarian—that he began to elaborate further and then to summarize some of his more important distinctions between the faith of a servant and the faith of a child of God. For example, in his sermon "On Faith" (1788), Wesley revealed, in part, what constitutes the difference between a servant and a child of God: "He that believeth as a child of God 'hath the witness in himself.' This the servant hath not."[42] Beyond this, Wesley maintained that one who is a servant of God, who "feareth God and worketh righteousness," enjoys the favor of God and is, therefore, accepted "to a degree." This is illustrated in his sermon "On Friendship with the World": "Those on the contrary 'are of God' who love God, or at least 'fear him, and keep his commandments.' This is the lowest character of those that 'are of God,' who are not properly sons, but servants."[43]

Unfortunately, early in his ministry, John Wesley had not fully appreciated the notion that those who "fear God and work righteousness" are indeed accepted of him, and because of this failure, he and his brother Charles caused great harm among those who were attentive to early Methodist preaching. In 1788, reflecting on this regrettable situation, Wesley confessed,

> Indeed nearly fifty years ago, when the preachers commonly called Methodists began to preach that grand scriptural doctrine, salvation by faith, they were not sufficiently apprised of the difference

between a servant and a child of God. They did not clearly understand that even one "who feared God, and worketh righteousness,
is accepted of him."[44]

Observe in these preceding reflections, then, that Wesley held
two ideas together, both important elements of his "conjunctive"
theology: on the one hand, he or she who fears God and works
righteousness is not a rank unbeliever, but on the other hand, "One
that fears God is [still] waiting for His salvation."[45] Indeed, late in
his career, Wesley continued to associate the faith of a servant, in a
broad sense, not with justification but with the spirit of bondage.
Additional evidence of this link is found in a letter to Thomas
Davenport (1781), in which Wesley counseled:

> You are in the hands of a wise Physician, who is lancing your sores
> in order to heal them. He has *given* you now *the spirit of fear.* But it is
> in order to *the spirit of love and of a sound mind.* You have now *received*
> *the spirit of bondage.* Is it not the forerunner of the Spirit of adoption?
> He is not afar off. Look up! And expect Him to cry in your heart,
> Abba, Father! He is nigh that justifieth![46]

This excerpt demonstrates quite clearly that in this late period
Wesley still did not confuse the issue of "acceptance" (for the light
and grace which they have) with justification, for those under "the
spirit of fear" are still waiting for the One who justifies. This
means, of course, that these believers are in the way of salvation;
consequently, if they continue in this grace—and unfortunately
some will not—then the One "who is nigh" will justify.

For Wesley, then, the servants of God in a broad sense obviously lack what he termed "the proper Christian faith"—and hence
cannot enjoy the privileges of the sons and daughters of God—yet
they have a measure of faith which arises from the prevenient
grace which precedes it and are *for that reason* not to be discouraged. Thus, Wesley's seasoned and relatively favorable estimation
of the faith of a servant in this sense probably emerged from his
consideration that such a faith, in the normal course of spiritual
development, would in time become the faith of a child of God. In
fact, in his sermon "On Faith" (1788), Wesley highlighted just such
a consideration: "And, indeed, unless the servants of God halt by

the way, they will receive the adoption of sons. They will receive the faith of the children of God by his revealing his only-begotten Son in their hearts.... And whosoever hath this, the Spirit of God witnesseth with his spirit that he is a child of God."[47] Likewise, Wesley's appreciation of a degree of acceptance and his exhortation to servants to improve the rich grace of God is revealed in a sermon of 1788, "On the Discoveries of Faith":

> Whoever has attained this, the faith of a servant,...in consequence of which he is *in a degree* (as the Apostle observes), "accepted with him."...Nevertheless he should be exhorted not to stop there; not to rest till he attains the adoption of sons; till he obeys out of love, which is the privilege of all the *children* of God.[48]

Simply put, the faith of a servant of God is valued not only for the measure of faith that it is, but also for what it will soon become: the qualitatively different faith of a child of God, where faith will be filled not with the energy of fear but with the energy of love.

During the 1780s the elderly Wesley was still at it—refining, nuancing, and offering further elaborations on his important distinction between the faith of a servant and the faith of a child of God; considering, in other words, what it meant to be a real Christian. As Wesley in his later years feared that the Methodists might be corrupted by riches, so too did he fear that they might rest content with a measure of grace far below the *common* privileges of the sons and daughters of God, that they might have the *form* of religion without its *power.* Such a fear and concern was yet another way in which Wesley underscored the importance of holy love, the eminent value of faith working by love, which is the very substance of redemption.

10

God Is with Us

In the early part of 1790 Wesley wrote "The Wedding Garment," a sermon that epitomized some of the leading themes of Methodism throughout the years. For one, it underscored the necessity of personal holiness to qualify believers for heaven and to make them fit for glory. Thus, even at this late date, Wesley yet feared that an erroneous notion of faith might make the law of love void among some of his people, that the "righteousness of Christ," which is imputed to believers, might be misunderstood as a substitute for personal holiness. Second, in this sermon Wesley pointed out once again that orthodoxy is a small part of religion and must not be mistaken for the very substance of the Christian faith, which is not a string of ideas or speculation of any sort, but holy love reigning in the heart.

Remarkably, Wesley distinguished holiness, which is itself the wedding garment, even from some of the General Rules of the United Societies, lest the Methodists be content with the mere form, the shell, of the Christian faith. Thus, Wesley underscored a difference between holiness and "avoiding evil," and then, second, between holiness and "doing good." Concerning the former, he pointed out "how many take holiness and harmlessness to mean one and the same thing! Whereas were a man as harmless as a post he might be as far from holiness as heaven from earth." And with respect to the latter, he reasoned, "Yea, suppose a person of this amiable character to do much good wherever he is, to feed the hungry, clothe the naked, relieve the stranger, the sick, the prisoner, yea, and to save many souls from death: it is possible he may still fall far short of that holiness without which he cannot see the Lord."[1] Clearly, then, the notion that any work, however noble, supersedes the necessity of holiness is the "very marrow of antinomianism," the substance of that which makes void the holy law of love. The importance of *doing* must not displace the *cruciality* of *being*.

Beyond this, Wesley's reading of à Kempis, Pascal, and Fenelon—judging from his comments in April of this same year[2]—convinced him of the inestimable value of the soul. In a letter to William Black a few months later, Wesley noted that "one soul is worth all the merchandise in the world."[3] This accent on the vitality of the soul and the significance of inward religion continued in Wesley's ministry, though he was, from time to time, criticized quite sharply for precisely these themes by those who were either outright ignorant of such matters or who thought all of this to be irrelevant, extravagant, and at best a pious indulgence. Joseph Humphreys, for example, who in 1738 was the first lay preacher to assist Wesley in England, actually scoffed at inward religion in his later years and when he was reminded of his own earlier experience the one-time disciple replied, "That was one of the foolish things which I wrote in the time of my madness."[4]

Unperturbed by such criticism, Wesley continued to highlight the value of inward religion in his later years in two key ways; first, by emphasizing his well-worked theme of real Christianity; and second, by showing the necessity of "going on to perfection." Concerning the former, in writing to his niece Sarah in August 1790, Wesley linked "perpetual cheerfulness" with the "temper of a Christian." "Real Christians know it is their duty to maintain this," Wesley observed, "which is in our sense to rejoice evermore."[5] Moreover, the previous month Wesley had affirmed that unless believers have "new senses, ideas, passions, [and] tempers, they are no Christians! However just, true, or merciful they may be, they are but atheists still."[6] And when Wesley preached his very last open-air sermon in the fields at Winchelsea in October 1790, it was none other than the words of real Christianity that were on his lips:

> I went over to that poor skeleton of ancient Winchelsea....I stood under a large tree, on the side of it, and called to most of the inhabitants of the town, "The kingdom of heaven is at hand; repent, and believe the gospel." It seemed as if all that heard were, for the present, almost persuaded to be Christians.[7]

Concerning the second emphasis, Christian perfection, Wesley continued to underscore its salience in his later years, for in his estimation it was a doctrine pivotal to growth in grace, a lure to spiritual betterment. He had affirmed to Robert Hopkins that "you will never find more life in your own soul than when you are earnestly exhorting others to go on to perfection."[8] Wesley was apparently very guarded, however, concerning his own experience: "I speak of myself very little," he had written to Sarah Crosby a decade earlier, "were it only for fear of hurting *them*. I have found exceeding few that could bear it; so I am constrained to repress my natural openness."[9] Was this an allusion to Wesley's own perfection of love? Was this a hint at his entire sanctification? The reference is not at all clear.

What is certain is that Wesley in his later years—especially during the decade of the 1780s—began to employ a slightly different idiom in urging the Methodists on to perfection. Mindful of the genius of the Protestant heritage, which Peter Böhler had communicated to him so many years before, a heritage which underscored the sheer gratuity of grace, Wesley urged several of his people to look for the promise of perfect love by what he termed "naked faith." In a letter to Robert Brackenbury on September 18, 1780, he pointed out, "If you look for it [Christian perfection] by naked faith, why may you not receive it now."[10] Five years later Wesley likewise encouraged Ann Loxdale to return to her first love: "You unquestionably did enjoy a measure of His pure and perfect love. And as you received it at first by naked faith, just so you may receive it again; and who knows how soon?"[11] And the following year, Wesley pointed out to Mrs. Bowman, "Expect continually the end of your faith, the full salvation of your soul. You know, whenever it is given, it is to be received only by naked faith."[12]

Wesley could counsel along these lines because he realized that if believers were waiting for something to be done first, if they wanted "to add" something to simple, gracious faith, then they were actually expecting sanctification by works, a clear impossibility. To clarify this issue, Wesley had observed much earlier in his summary sermon, "The Scripture Way of Salvation":

> And by this token you may surely know whether you seek it by faith or by works. If by works, you want something to be done *first,*

before you are sanctified. You think, "I must first *be* or *do* thus or thus." Then you are seeking it by works unto this day. If you seek it by faith, you may expect it *as you are:* and if as you are, then expect it now.[13]

In these comments, Wesley was not slighting the means of grace such as praying, receiving the Lord's Supper, and reading the Bible. Nevertheless, though such channels would normally be the means through which sanctifying grace was received, Wesley insisted that these means could never be the *basis* upon which such grace was received. The difference was important.

In September 1790, Wesley referred to Christian perfection as "the grand depositum which God has lodged with the people called Methodists," and he maintained that "for the sake of propagating this chiefly He appeared to have raised us up."[14] But this forthright assertion must not be taken to mean that Wesley viewed Christian perfection as a Methodist distinctive, as if it were a denominational marker. Such a provincial view would have invariably marked defeat for Methodism—and Wesley clearly knew this. The doctrine of perfect love belonged not simply to the Methodists but to the whole church, to the universal community of faith. In April 1790, for example, Wesley had cautioned, "The Methodists are to spread life among *all* denominations; which they will do till they form a separate sect."[15] Thus, the ecclesiastical question of whether Methodism would remain in the church, which had preoccupied Wesley throughout the years, was actually connected to the very purpose of Methodism in the first place: namely, to spread scriptural holiness across the land, to be a witness not simply among themselves but to give evidence to all people, to Anglicans, Moravians, Calvinists, Roman Catholics, and others, of the remarkable value of holy love. It was, therefore, to maintain the *universality* of this witness that Wesley had urged his people not to depart from the church. Little wonder that he (and his brother) had been so concerned about this issue.

In 1790, Wesley was also concerned, however, with the other half of the equation, not that the Methodists would leave the church but that they would be cast out or at least frustrated in their ongoing mission by a hostile or indifferent clergy. In June, for example, he asked the Bishop of Lincoln, Dr. Pretyman Tomline, "For what reasonable end would your Lordship drive these people out of the Church?" "And is it a Christian, yea a Protestant bishop," Wesley continued, "that so persecutes his own flock?"[16] The following month, a few days after Wesley's last Conference, which was held in Bristol, he wrote to William Wilberforce, reformer and states-man, "Now sir, what can the Methodists do? They are liable to be ruined by the Conventicle Act, and they have no relief from the Act of Toleration! If this is not oppression, what is?"[17]

Correspondence with Wilberforce during this period reveals that Wesley was not simply concerned with the plight of the Methodists and religious liberty in particular, but also with other basic human rights such as personal liberty (or the lack thereof) with respect to the wretched institution of slavery. Thus, shortly before his death, Wesley again wrote to Wilberforce, who was a member of Parliament at the time, urging him to continue his reforming, abolitionist efforts: "O be not weary of well doing! Go on, in the name of God and in the power of His might, till even American slavery (the vilest that ever saw the sun) shall vanish away before it."[18] A few years earlier, Wesley had corresponded with Granville Sharp, who had founded a society for abolition of slavery in 1787, and noted that "ever since I heard of it...I felt a perfect detestation of the horrid slave trade, but more particularly since I had the pleasure of reading what you have published upon the subject."[19] Beyond this, a month later in November 1787, Wesley revealed similar sentiments to Thomas Funnell. "Whatever assistance I can give those generous men who join to oppose that execrable trade I certainly shall give. I have printed a large edition on the *Thoughts on Slavery.*"[20] Clearly, then, in Wesley's eyes, the ongoing practice of slavery was nothing less than a scandal, "not only to Christianity but [to] humanity [as well]."[21]

Interestingly, it was not really any political philosophy which had led Wesley to such judgments on slavery. Rather, it was some of Wesley's own theological concerns expressed in his attentive-ness to the moral law, that "copy of the divine mind," that actual-ly confirmed him in his views. Put another way, the moral law, which expresses the "fitness of relations" between God and humanity, was an "objective" standard that Wesley could appeal to, above the pull and tug of unjust laws and political pressures, to ensure that all human beings, ever created in the image and likeness of God, were not denied precisely what belonged to them *as* human beings, the right of liberty among these. Wesley's life and witness, then, informed by sophisticated theological reasoning, was surely an encouragement to Wilberforce, Shaftsbury, and others as they helped to turn back this "execrable trade" in Britain.

Though Wesley was characteristically concerned with the plight of others in the early days of 1790, his own physical need was great. By now his strength had nearly abandoned him, the optimistic references to his health in the journal were all gone, and he slowed down considerably. He was, quite simply, an old man on the doors of eternity, his strength spent in the rounds of ministry. "Time has shaken me by the hand," Wesley wrote to Freeborn Garrettson in February 1790, "and death is not far behind."[22] The nearly worn-out preacher had noted a sudden change in his condition earlier, in August 1789, when his eyes became dim and his strength left him.[23] Wesley's great fear, given the nature of his life, was that he would live to be useless.[24] "I am half blind and half lame" he related to Thomas Greathead in January 1791, yet he took some comfort in noting, "but by the help of God I creep on still."[25] The following month, Wesley knew the end was approaching and so he wrote to Ezekiel Cooper that "those [who] desire to write or say anything to me have no time to lose."[26] Wesley preached his last sermon, at Leatherhead, toward the end of February with a disposition marked by seasoned grace. It had been a long career, spanning much of the eighteenth century, and it was now drawing to a close.

Wesley was back in City Road, London, by Friday, February 25. Elizabeth Ritchie, a friend, was concerned as she watched the elderly gentleman step down from the coach. Ill from a fever that arose a day earlier, Wesley immediately went to bed and asked to be left alone for half an hour. He remained bed-ridden over the weekend. By Monday his weakness had increased and his friends became alarmed. That evening, Wesley had a very restless night, but when he was asked whether he was in pain, he replied "No." On Tuesday, March 1, Wesley was sinking. He called on Mr. Bradford to give him a pen and ink, but he could no longer write. Elizabeth Ritchie, who was at his side, replied, "Let me write for you, sir; tell me what you would say." "Nothing," Wesley spoke, "but that God is with us."[27] In the afternoon, Wesley got up, and to the astonishment of all, given his condition, he broke out in the words of a hymn by Isaac Watts:

> I'll praise my Maker while I've breath,
> And when my voice is lost in death,
>   Praise shall employ my nobler powers:
> My days of praise shall ne'er be past,
> While life, and thought, and being last,
>   Or immortality endures.
>
> Happy the man whose hopes rely
> On Israel's God; He made the sky,
>   And earth, and seas with all their train;
> His truth for ever stands secure,
> He saves th' oppressed, He feeds the poor,
>   And none shall find His promise vain.[28]

Dr. Whitehead, Elizabeth Ritchie, Charles Wesley's widow and daughter, as well as about nine others were present in the room. Wesley gathered his strength once more and cried out, "The best of all, God is with us!" The dying saint lingered throughout the night often repeating the lines from Watts' hymn, "I'll praise; I'll praise." The following morning, March 2, Wesley uttered his last word, "Farewell!" and died "without a struggle or a groan," at about 10:00 A.M.

As Wesley closed his eyes that March morning, there were nearly three hundred preachers in Britain alone and over 70,000 members. The Methodist classes, bands, and the select societies would soon meet; the poor would receive both spiritual and material care; and the common people would hear the glad tidings of salvation in chapels as in the fields. Lending stocks, loans, a medical dispensary, and even a Stranger's society, which ministered to the forgotten of England, had been a part of this considerable legacy. Penny tracts and the publication of Wesley's sermons made their contribution as well. And though Wesley himself offered no profession of perfect love, not even on his deathbed, he could take comfort in a life well lived in service to both God and neighbor: he had traveled over a quarter of a million miles, preached more than forty thousand sermons, and had written more than two hundred books.

Wesley's real comfort, however, and his sure source of strength, was not in anything he had done, no matter how noble or sacrificial. His comfort remained in what God had graciously done for him in Jesus Christ by forgiving his sins and by empowering him for service. In the end, Wesley died as he had lived for so long, not as a perfect Christian, not as one who in each instance exercised the very best judgment, but as one who gave an enduring testimony, a faithful witness, by his thoughts as by his actions, of the remarkable grace and high honor of having lived as nothing less than a real Christian—a real Christian indeed.

NOTES

CHAPTER 1. THE FAMILY CIRCLE

1. W. H. Fitchett, *Wesley and His Century: A Study in Spiritual Forces* (London: Smith, Elder, & Co., 1906), p. 57.

2. Rebecca Lamar Harmon, *Susanna: Mother of the Wesleys* (Nashville: Abingdon Press, 1984), p. 47.

3. Some well-known biographies insist that Wesley was born on June 17, 1703, while others maintain a date of June 28, 1703. Why the discrepancy? Julius Caesar effected the first reform of the Western calendar in 45 B.C. An improvement over the previous reckoning, this calendar determined the year to be 365 and 1/4 days and, therefore, added an additional day every four years (a leap year). The problem with the Julian calendar, however, was that the earth takes slightly fewer than 365 and 1/4 days to revolve around the sun. The difference is small, but by the sixteenth century, a shift of seven days in every thousand years left Pope Gregory XIII ten days off and having to reckon the date of Easter.

The commission Gregory appointed to study the problem arrived at a new formula, which became the Gregorian calendar. Like the Julian calendar, a day would be added every fourth year, with an important exception: Leap years would be removed at century marks (1700, 1800, etc.), but would be reinstated at century marks divisible by 400 (1200, 1600, 2000, etc.). Thus, this reform made an adjustment to the Julian calendar by dropping three days every four centuries and is accurate to the rate of one day off every 2,800 years. Not again until the year 4382 will the calendar need correcting by one day.

Thus, during his lifetime, and because the British did not adopt the Gregorian calendar until 1752, Wesley's birthday emerged as June 28, not June 17. In later life, Wesley celebrated his birthday (usually with boasts about his excellent health) on June 28.

4. Maldwyn Edwards, *Family Circle* (London: Epworth Press, 1961), p. 20.

5. Leslie Church, *Knight of the Burning Heart* (London: Epworth Press, 1938), pp. 15-16.

6. Frank Baker, ed., *The Works of John Wesley*, Bicentennial ed., vol. 25, *Letters* (Nashville: Abingdon Press, 1980), 330-31.

7. Reginald W. Ward and Richard P. Heitzenrater, eds., *The Works of John Wesley*, Bicentennial ed., vol. 19, *Journal and Diaries II* (Nashville: Abingdon Press, 1990), 290-91 (here abridged).

8. Robert Southey, *The Life of Wesley; and Rise and Progress of Methodism,* vol. 1 (London: Longman, Brown, Green, and Longmans, 1846), p. 14.

9. John Telford, *The Life of John Wesley* (London: Wesleyan Methodist Book Room, 1899), pp. 19-20, emphasis added.

10. Maldwyn Edwards, *John Wesley,* 4th ed. (Madison, N.J.: General Commission on Archives, 1987), p. 15.

11. Harmon, *Susanna,* p. 80.

12. Ward and Heitzenrater, *Journals and Diaries,* 18:243.

13. Luke Tyerman, *The Life and Times of the Rev. John Wesley, M.A.,* 3 vols. (New York: Burt Franklin, 1872), 1:22.

14. Telford, *Life of John Wesley,* p. 30.

15. Ibid.

16. Church, *Burning Heart,* p. 31.

17. Baker, *Letters,* 25:148.

18. Telford, *Life of John Wesley,* p. 33.

CHAPTER 2. THE POINT OF IT ALL

1. Luke Tyerman, *The Life and Times of the Rev. John Wesley, M.A.,* 3 vols. (New York: Burt Franklin, 1872), 1:33.

2. Frank Baker, *The Works of John Wesley,* Bicentennial ed., vol. 25, *Letters* (Nashville: Abingdon Press, 1980), 149.

3. Ibid., 160.

4. W. H. Fitchett, *Wesley and His Century: A Study in Spiritual Forces* (London: Smith, Elder & Co., 1906), p. 62.

5. Baker, *Letters,* 25:160.

6. Ibid., 158.

7. Ibid., 160.

8. Ibid.

9. W. Reginald Ward and Richard P. Heitzenrater, eds., *The Works of John Wesley,* Bicentennial ed., vol. 18, *Journals and Diaries* (Nashville: Abingdon Press, 1988), 244.

10. Ibid., 244 n. 37.

11. Thomas Jackson, ed., *The Works of John Wesley,* 14 vols. (Grand Rapids, Mich.: Baker Book House, 1978), 11:366-67.

12. Ibid., 11:366.

13. Albert C. Outler, ed., *The Works of John Wesley,* Bicentennial ed., vols. 1–4, *The Sermons* (Nashville: Abingdon Press, 1984), 3:152.

14. Tyerman, *Life and Times,* 1:31.

15. Baker, *Letters,* 25:175-76.

16. Ibid., 179.

17. Ibid., 188.

18. Ibid., 194.

19. Ibid., 208.

20. John Telford, ed., *The Letters of the Rev. John Wesley,* 8 vols. (London: Epworth Press, 1931), 1:39.

21. Baker, *Letters*, 25:208-9.

22. Jackson, *Works*, 11:367.

23. Ward and Heitzenrater, *Journals and Diaries*, 18:244-45.

24. Baker, *Letters*, 25:240.

25. Outler, *Sermons*, 3:581.

26. John Telford, *The Life of John Wesley* (London: Wesleyan Methodist Book Room, 1899), pp. 58-59.

27. Ibid.

28. J. H. Overton, *John Wesley* (London: Methuen and Co., 1891), p. 28 n. 1. Heitzenrater points out that "the first contemporary reference to the term comes in a letter from John Clayton, at Oxford, to John Wesley, visiting London in August 1732." Cf. Richard P. Heitzenrater, *Wesley and the People Called Methodists* (Nashville: Abingdon Press, 1995), pp. 45-46.

29. Outler, *Sermons*, 3:275-76.

30. Jackson, *Works*, 11:367.

31. Outler, *Sermons*, 3:504.

32. Baker, *Letters*, 25:293.

33. Baker, *Letters*, 25:365.

34. Heitzenrater, *Wesley and the People Called Methodists*, p. 52.

35. Baker, *Letters*, 25:366.

36. Ibid., 369.

37. V. H. H. Green, *John Wesley* (Lanham, Md.: University Press of America, 1987; reprint of 1964 ed.), p. 17.

38. John Pollock, *John Wesley* (Oxford, England: Lion Publishing, 1989), p. 40.

39. Ibid., p. 39.

40. Ibid.

41. Baker, *Letters*, 25:329.

42. Outler, *Sermons*, 1:402-3.

43. Baker, *Letters*, 25:395.

44. Ibid., 396.

45. Ibid., 411.

46. Ibid., 420.

47. Ibid., 421.

48. Ibid., 399.

49. Ibid., 400.

50. Cf. Richard Heitzenrater's essay, "Great Expectations: Aldersgate and the Evidences of Genuine Christianity," in Randy L. Maddox, ed., *Aldersgate Reconsidered* (Nashville: Kingswood Books, 1990), p. 61.

CHAPTER 3. THE EDUCATION OF A VIRTUOUS AND AFFECTIONATE MAN

1. Maldwyn Edwards, *Family Circle* (London: Epworth Press, 1961), p. 32.

2. Frank Baker, *The Works of John Wesley*, Bicentennial ed., vol. 25, *Letters* (Nashville: Abingdon Press, 1980), 439.

3. Reginald W. Ward and Richard P. Heitzenrater, eds., *The Works of John Wesley*, Bicentennial ed., vol. 18, *Journals and Diaries* (Nashville: Abingdon Press, 1988), 140.

4. Ibid., 18:141.

5. Ibid., 142.

6. Ibid., 143.

7. Ibid.

8. Ibid., 165.

9. Ibid., 169.

10. John Telford, ed., *The Letters of John Wesley, A.M.*, 8 vols. (London: Epworth Press, 1931), 6:30-31, emphasis added.

11. Ward and Heitzenrater, *Journals and Diaries*, 18:140.

12. Ibid., 155.

13. Ibid., 146.

14. W. H. Fitchett, *Wesley and His Century: A Study in Spiritual Forces* (London: Smith, Elder, & Co., 1906), p. 102.

15. Ward and Heitzenrater, *Journal and Diaries*, 18:162.

16. V. H. H. Green, *John Wesley* (Lanham, Md.: University Press of America, 1987), p. 45.

17. Ward and Heitzenrater, *Journal and Diaries*, 18:516.

18. Ibid., 435.

19. Ibid., 436.

20. Ibid., 438.

21. Ibid., 442.

22. Ibid., 469.

23. Ibid., 470.

24. Ibid., 471.

25. Ibid., 476, 477.

26. Ibid., 477, 478.

27. Ibid., 480.

28. Ibid., 482.

29. Ibid., 482-83.

30. Ibid., 485.

31. Ibid., 486.

32. Ibid., 490.

33. Ibid., 184.

34. Ibid., 188.

35. Ibid., 193.

36. Ibid., 195.

37. Ibid., 207.

38. Ibid., 208-9.

39. Ibid., 209. The Latin translates, "Let life be a burden to me."

40. Ibid., 211.

41. Ibid., 213.

CHAPTER 4. THE MAKINGS OF A SAINT

1. Reginald W. Ward and Richard P. Heitzenrater, eds., *The Works of John Wesley*, Bicentennial ed., vol. 18, *Journals and Diaries* (Nashville: Abingdon Press, 1988), 214.

2. Ibid., 214-15.

3. Ibid., 215.

4. Ibid., 215-16.

5. Ibid., 221.

6. Ibid., 223.

7. Ibid., 226.

8. Ibid., 228.

9. Ibid., 233-34.

10. Ibid., 234.

11. Robert Southey, *The Life of Wesley; and Rise and Progress of Methodism*, vol. 1 (London: Longman, Brown, Green, and Longmans, 1846), p. 134.

12. Ward and Heitzenrater, *Journals and Diaries*, 18:236.

13. Albert C. Outler, ed., *The Works of John Wesley*, Bicentennial ed., vols. 1–4, *Sermons* (Nashville: Abingdon Press, 1984–87), 1:533.

14. Ward and Heitzenrater, *Journals and Diaries*, 18:235.

15. Frank Baker, ed., *The Works of John Wesley*, Bicentennial ed., vol. 25, *Letters* (Nashville: Abingdon Press, 1980), 541.

16. Ibid.

17. Ibid., 542.

18. Ward and Heitzenrater, *Journals and Diaries*, 18:237.

19. Thomas Jackson, ed., *The Journals of Rev. Charles Wesley*, 2 vols. (London: John Mason, 1849; Grand Rapids, Mich.: Baker Book House, 1980), 1:88.

20. Ibid., 1:90.

21. Ibid., 1:91.

22. Baker, *Letters*, 26:183.

23. Ward and Heitzenrater, *Journals and Diaries*, 18:246.

24. Ibid., 247-48.

25. Ibid., 249.

26. Ibid., 249-50.

27. Ibid., 250-53.

28. Outler, *Sermons*, 1:121.

29. Ibid., 124.

30. Thomas Jackson, ed., *The Works of John Wesley*, 14 vols. (Grand Rapids, Mich.: Baker Book House, 1978), 10:364.

31. Ward and Heitzenrater, *Journals and Diaries*, 18:216, emphasis added.

32. Outler, *Sermons*, 1:137-39.

33. Ward and Heitzenrater, *Journals and Diaries*, 18:260.

34. Ibid., 19:18.

35. Ibid., 18:254.

36. Ibid., 19:19.

37. John Telford, ed., *The Letters of the Rev. John Wesley*, 8 vols. (London: Epworth Press, 1931), 1:258.
38. Baker, *Letters*, 25:576-77.
39. Ibid., 575.
40. Ibid., 598.
41. Ward and Heitzenrater, *Journals and Diaries*, 19:21.
42. Ibid., 22.
43. Ibid., 46.
44. Baker, *Letters*, 25:616.
45. Ward and Heitzenrater, *Journals and Diaries*, 19:51.

CHAPTER 5. METHODISM DISTINGUISHED

1. W. Reginald Ward and Richard P. Heitzenrater, *The Works of John Wesley*, Bicentennial ed., vol. 19, *Journals and Diaries* (Nashville: Abingdon Press, 1990), 64.
2. Ibid.
3. Ibid., 70.
4. Frank Baker, ed., *The Works of John Wesley*, Bicentennial ed., vol. 25, *Letters* (Nashville: Abingdon Press, 1980), 694-95.
5. Ibid., 660.
6. Ibid.
7. Ibid., 26:237.
8. Ward and Heitzenrater, *Journals and Diaries*, 19:96.
9. Ibid., 106.
10. Richard P. Heitzenrater, *Wesley and the People Called Methodists* (Nashville: Abingdon Press, 1995), p. 115.
11. Gerald R. Cragg, ed., *The Works of John Wesley*, Bicentennial ed., vol. 11, *Appeals to Men of Reason and Religion and Certain Related Open Letters* (Nashville: Abingdon Press, 1975), 29.
12. Ward and Heitzenrater, *Journals and Diaries*, 19:130.
13. Ibid., 132.
14. Ibid., 147.
15. Ibid., 161.
16. Ibid., 191.
17. Ibid., 190.
18. Ibid., 213-14.
19. Ibid., 195.
20. Ibid., 18:216.
21. Ibid., 20:88-89.
22. Ibid., 19:180 n. 13.
23. Ibid., 188-89.
24. Baker, *Letters*, 26:32.
25. Robert Southey, *The Life of Wesley; and Rise and Progress of Methodism*, vol. 1 (London: Longman, Brown, Green, and Longmans, 1846), p. 314.

26. Baker, *Letters,* 26:32.

27. Ibid., 54.

28. Albert C. Outler, ed., *The Works of John Wesley,* vols. 1–4, *The Sermons* (Nashville: Abingdon Press, 1984), 2:105.

29. Ibid., 1:419.

30. Ward and Heitzenrater, *Journals and Diaries,* 19:260.

31. Ibid., 283.

32. Ibid., 283-84.

33. Arnold A. Dallimore, *Susanna Wesley: The Mother of John and Charles Wesley* (Grand Rapids, Mich.: Baker Book House, 1993), p. 162.

34. Rupert E. Davies, ed., *The Works of John Wesley,* Bicentennial ed., vol. 9, *The Methodist Societies* (Nashville: Abingdon Press, 1989), 222-23.

35. Ibid., 69.

36. D. Michael Henderson, *John Wesley's Class Meeting: A Model for Making Disciples* (Nappanee, Ind.: Evangel Publishing House, 1997), p. 83.

37. Ibid., pp. 97-98.

38. Ibid., p. 47.

39. Davies, *Societies,* 9:69.

40. Ward and Heitzenrater, *Journals and Diaries,* 19:318.

41. Henderson, *Class Meeting,* p. 30.

42. Ward and Heitzenrater, *Journals and Diaries,* 19:346.

43. Ibid., 20:76.

44. Cragg, *Appeals,* 11:33.

45. Ibid., 14.

46. Ibid., 30.

47. Ward and Heitzenrater, *Journals and Diaries,* 20:407.

48. Cragg, *Appeals,* 11:14.

49. Ibid., 35.

50. Ibid., 39.

51. Outler, *Sermons,* 1:179.

52. Ward and Heitzenrater, *Journals and Diaries,* 20:36-37.

53. Thomas Jackson, ed., *The Works of John Wesley,* 14 vols. (Grand Rapids, Mich.: Baker Book House, 1978), 8:287-88.

54. Ibid., 288-89.

55. In particular, the identification of the "faith of a servant" with the "spirit of bondage" is revealed in the late sermon, "The Discoveries of Faith" (1788). In it, Wesley observes, "Exhort him to press on by all possible means, till he passes 'from faith to faith'; from the faith of a *servant* to the faith of a *son;* from the *spirit of bondage* unto fear, to the spirit of childlike love." Cf. Albert C. Outler, ed., *The Works of John Wesley,* vols. 1–4, *The Sermons* (Nashville: Abingdon Press, 1984), 4:35-36.

56. Outler, *Sermons,* 1:258.

57. Baker, *Letters,* 25:575.

58. Richard P. Heitzenrater, "Great Expectations: Aldersgate and the Evidences of Genuine Christianity," in *Aldersgate Reconsidered,* ed. Randy L. Maddox (Nashville: Kingswood Books, 1990), p. 89.

59. Baker, *Letters*, 26:107-8.
60. Jackson, *Wesley's Works*, 8:276, emphasis added.
61. Ibid., 8:282.
62. Ibid., 8:293.
63. Ibid.
64. Baker, *Letters*, 26:182, emphasis mine.
65. Ibid., 26:246.
66. Ibid., 26:254-55.
67. Outler, *Sermons*, 1:177.

CHAPTER 6. SETTLING DOWN

1. Reginald W. Ward and Richard P. Heitzenrater, eds., *The Works of John Wesley*, Bicentennial ed., vol. 20, *Journals and Diaries* (Nashville: Abingdon Press, 1991), 445.
2. Ibid., 156.
3. Arnold Lunn, *John Wesley* (New York: Dial Press, 1929), p. 205.
4. Ward and Heitzenrater, *Journals and Diaries*, 20:340.
5. Ibid., 432.
6. Cf. Richard P. Heitzenrater, *Wesley and the People Called Methodists* (Nashville: Abingdon Press, 1995), p. 203.
7. Rupert E. Davies, *The Works of John Wesley*, vol. 9, *The Methodist Societies: History, Nature, and Design* (Nashville: Abingdon Press, 1989), p. 254.
8. Ibid., 258-59.
9. Frank Baker, ed., *The Works of John Wesley*, Bicentennial ed., vol. 26, *Letters* (Nashville: Abingdon Press, 1982), 505.
10. Ward and Heitzenrater, *Journals and Diaries*, 18:472.
11. Hardwicke's Act was passed a few years later in 1753 in order to rectify these problems. This Act declared, quite simply, that henceforth "no marriage was valid unless performed after banns or by licence." Cf. John Pollock, *John Wesley* (Oxford, England: Lion Publishing, 1989), p. 193.
12. Cf. L. Tyerman, *The Life and Times of the Rev. John Wesley, M.A.*, 3 vols. (New York: Burt Franklin, 1872), 2:51.
13. Ibid.
14. Baker, *Letters*, 26:389.
15. Ward and Heitzenrater, *Journals and Diaries*, 20:300 n. 41.
16. Pollock, *John Wesley*, p. 204.
17. Baker, *Letters*, 26:451.
18. Ward and Heitzenrater, *Journals and Diaries*, 20:378 n. 51.
19. Baker, *Letters*, 26:455.
20. Ibid., 457.
21. Ibid., 456.
22. Ibid., 462.
23. Ibid., 454.

24. Stanley Ayling, *John Wesley* (New York: William Collins Publishers, 1979; Nashville: Abingdon, 1981), p. 224.

25. John Telford, ed., *The Letters of the Rev. John Wesley,* 8 vols. (London: Epworth Press, 1931), 4:4.

26. Ibid., 3:180.

27. Baker, *Letters,* 26:494.

28. Telford, *Letters,* 2:148.

29. Ward and Heitzenrater, *Journals and Diaries,* 21:20.

30. Telford, *Letters,* 2:148.

31. Robert Southey, *The Life of Wesley; and Rise and Progress of Methodism,* vol. 2 (London: Longman, Brown, Green, and Longmans, 1846), p. 191.

32. Lunn, *John Wesley,* pp. 188-89.

33. Telford, *Letters,* 3:186.

34. Baker, *Letters,* 26:601-2.

35. Telford, *Letters,* 3:289.

36. Baker, *Letters,* 26:491.

37. Ibid.

38. Ibid., 26:424.

39. John Wesley, *Explanatory Notes Upon the New Testament* (Salem, Ohio: Schmul Publishers), p. 73.

40. Baker, *Letters,* 26:425.

41. Ward and Heitzenrater, *Journals and Diaries,* 21:123.

42. Ibid., 20:489.

43. Telford, *Letters,* 3:183.

44. Ward and Heitzenrater, *Journals and Diaries,* 20:356.

45. Ward and Heitzenrater, *Journals and Diaries,* 21:10.

46. Baker, *Letters,* 26:609.

47. Ward and Heitzenrater, *Journals and Diaries,* 21:77.

48. Albert C. Outler, ed., *The Works of John Wesley,* vols. 1–4, *The Sermons* (Nashville: Abingdon Press, 1984), 1:572.

49. Wesley, *NT Notes,* p. 127.

50. Ibid., p. 351.

51. Ibid., p. 382.

52. Ibid., p. 49.

53. Ibid., p. 304, emphasis added.

54. Baker, *Letters,* 26:575.

Chapter 7. Challenges Without and Within

1. John Telford, ed., *The Letters of John Wesley, A.M.,* 8 vols. (London: Epworth Press, 1931), 4:150.

2. Ibid., 4:290.

3. Ibid., 4:99.

4. Ibid., 4:100.

5. Ibid., 4:147-48.

6. Reginald W. Ward and Richard P. Heitzenrater, eds., *The Works of John Wesley*, Bicentennial ed., vol. 21, *Journals and Diaries* (Nashville: Abingdon Press, 1992), 479.

7. Ibid., 22:8.

8. Telford, *Letters*, 4:339.

9. Ibid., 4:344.

10. Ibid., 4:342.

11. Ibid., 4:375.

12. Ibid., 4:380.

13. Ibid., 4:376.

14. Thomas Jackson, ed., *The Works of John Wesley*, 14 vols. (Grand Rapids, Mich.: Baker Book House, 1978), 10:365.

15. Ibid.

16. J. S. Simon, *John Wesley the Master Builder* (London: Epworth Press, 1927), p. 166.

17. Albert C. Outler, ed., *The Works of John Wesley*, Bicentennial ed., vols. 1–4, *Sermons* (Nashville: Abingdon Press, 1984), 1:445.

18. Outler, *Sermons*, 1:446.

19. Ward and Heitzenrater, *Journals and Diaries*, 22:29.

20. Telford, *Letters*, 5:69.

21. Ward and Heitzenrater, *Journals and Diaries*, 22:168, 172.

22. Telford, *Letters*, 4:52.

23. Ibid., 4:76.

24. Ibid., 4:77.

25. Ibid., 4:89.

26. Ibid., 4:143.

27. Ibid., 4:200.

28. Ibid., 4:265.

29. Ibid., 5:21.

30. Ibid., 5:105.

31. Outler, *Sermons*, 1:328.

32. Telford, *Letters*, 4:158.

33. Ibid., 4:187.

34. Ibid.

35. Ibid.

36. Ibid., 5:141.

37. Ward and Heitzenrater, *Journals and Diaries*, 22:22-23.

38. Telford, *Letters*, 4:321.

39. Ibid.

40. Ibid., 5:61.

41. Ibid., 5:83.

42. Ibid., 5:88.

43. Ibid., 5:93.

44. Ibid., 4:133.

45. Ibid., 4:186.

46. Ward and Heitzenrater, *Journals and Diaries*, 21:386.

47. Ibid., 21:474.

48. Telford, *Letters*, 5:20.

49. Ward and Heitzenrater, *Journals and Diaries*, 22:72.

50. Telford, *Letters*, 5:102.

51. Ward and Heitzenrater, *Journals and Diaries*, 21:398-99.

52. Ibid., 21:394.

53. Ibid., 21:403.

54. Ibid.

55. Ibid., 21:408.

56. Telford, *Letters*, 5:38.

57. Ibid., 4:120.

58. Ibid., 5:137.

59. Ibid., 4:263-64.

60. Ibid., 5:207.

61. Frank Baker, ed., *The Works of John Wesley*, Bicentennial ed., vols. 25, 26, *Letters* (Nashville: Abingdon Press, 1980, 1982), 26:575.

62. Ibid.

63. Ibid.

64. Ibid.

65. Outler, *Sermons*, 2:161.

66. Telford, *Letters*, 3:163.

67. Ibid., 5:358.

68. Wesley wrote to Dr. Rutherforth, "Therefore I have not for many years thought a consciousness of acceptance to be essential to justifying faith" (Telford, *Letters*, 5:359). See also Lycurgus M. Starkey, Jr., *The Work of the Holy Spirit: A Study in Wesleyan Theology* (Nashville/New York: Abingdon Press, 1962), pp. 68-69.

69. I have reversed the terminology used in my earlier book, *The Scripture Way of Salvation*. There the terms "broad" and "narrow" referred to whether or not the position included justification; that is, the terms did *not* refer to the *numbers* entailed. Though this was an apt distinction, I have reversed it here simply because most people invariably think of the *numbers* of people entailed—not whether the position *includes* or excludes justification—when the language of broad and narrow is used. Now the term "broad" means that the faith of a servant includes many people; "narrow" means it doesn't. This should bring greater clarity to the discussion.

70. Francis J. McConnell, *John Wesley* (New York: Abingdon Press, 1939), pp. 167-68.

71. Ibid.

72. Thomas Jackson, ed., *The Works of John Wesley*, 14 vols. (Grand Rapids, Mich.: Baker Book House, 1978), 4:469.

73. Outler, *Sermons*, 2:543.

Chapter 8. Fearing God and Honoring the King

1. Manfred Marquardt, *John Wesley's Social Ethics: Praxis and Principles* (Nashville: Abingdon Press, 1992), p. 29.

2. Reginald W. Ward and Richard P. Heitzenrater, eds., *The Works of John Wesley,* Bicentennial ed., vol. 22, *Journals and Diaries* (Nashville: Abingdon Press, 1993), 69.

3. John Telford, ed., *The Letters of John Wesley, A.M.,* 8 vols. (London: Epworth Press, 1931), 5:180.

4. Thomas Jackson, ed., *The Works of John Wesley,* 14 vols. (Grand Rapids, Mich.: Baker Book House, 1978), 11:57.

5. Telford, *Letters,* 6:161.

6. Ibid., 6:267.

7. Ibid., 6:192.

8. Jackson, *Wesley's Works,* 11:83.

9. Ibid., 11:84.

10. Ibid., 11:87.

11. Ibid., 11:105.

12. Telford, *Letters,* 6:102.

13. Ibid., 6:273-74.

14. Ibid. In this letter, John indicates that Mary has accused him of adultery—a charge which is utterly without foundation. For more on this allegation, cf. Henry D. Rack, *Reasonable Enthusiast: John Wesley and the Rise of Methodism,* 2nd ed. (Nashville: Abingdon Press, 1993), p. 266.

15. Ibid., 6:322.

16. Ibid., 6:368.

17. Robert Southey, *The Life of Wesley; and Rise and Progress of Methodism,* vol. 2 (London: Longman, Brown, Green, and Longmans, 1846), p. 245.

18. Telford, *Letters,* 5:192.

19. Ward and Heitzenrater, *Journals and Diaries,* 22:255.

20. Telford, *Letters,* 5:252.

21. Ibid., 5:231.

22. Ward and Heitzenrater, *Journals and Diaries,* 22:285.

23. Nolan Harmon, ed., *The Encyclopedia of World Methodism,* vol. 2 (Nashville: United Methodist Publishing House, 1974), p. 2146.

24. Ward and Heitzenrater, *Journals and Diaries,* 22:285-87 n. 42, emphasis added.

25. Harmon, *Encyclopedia,* 2:2146.

26. Telford, *Letters,* 5:274.

27. Ibid.

28. Ibid., 5:282.

29. Ward and Heitzenrater, *Journals and Diaries,* 23:56-57.

30. Jackson, *Wesley's Works,* 8:337.

31. Telford, *Letters,* 5:263.

32. Ibid., 5:197, emphasis added.

33. Ibid., 6:272-73, emphasis added.
34. Ibid., 6:51.
35. Ward and Heitzenrater, *Journals and Diaries*, 22:400.
36. Telford, *Letters*, 6:250.
37. Albert C. Outler, ed., *The Works of John Wesley*, Bicentennial ed., vols. 1–4, *The Sermons* (Nashville: Abingdon Press, 1984), 4:175.
38. Ward and Heitzenrater, *Journals and Diaries*, 22:367.
39. Telford, *Letters*, 6:201.
40. Ibid., 6:326-27.
41. Outler, *Sermons*, 2:385.
42. Harmon, *Encyclopedia*, 1:139-40.
43. Telford, *Letters*, 6:238.
44. Ward and Heitzenrater, *Journals and Diaries*, 23:111.

CHAPTER 9. BUILDING A LEGACY

1. John Telford, ed., *The Letters of John Wesley, A.M.*, 8 vols. (London: Epworth Press, 1931), 7:30.
2. Ibid., 7:30-31.
3. Ibid., 7:31.
4. Ibid., 7:239.
5. Ibid., 7:238.
6. Ibid., 7:262.
7. Ibid., 7:288.
8. Ibid., 8:91.
9. Ibid., 8:183.
10. Thomas Jackson, ed., *The Works of John Wesley*, 14 vols. (Grand Rapids, Mich.: Baker Book House, 1978), 8:319.
11. Telford, *Letters*, 8:66.
12. Ibid., 8:142.
13. Ibid., 8:92.
14. Nehemiah Curnock, ed., *The Journal of the Rev. John Wesley, A.M.*, 8 vols. (London: Epworth Press, 1938), 7:422, emphasis added.
15. Telford, *Letters*, 6:271-72.
16. Richard P. Heitzenrater, *Wesley and the People Called Methodists* (Nashville: Abingdon Press, 1995), p. 284.
17. Telford, *Letters*, 7:284.
18. V. H. H. Green, *John Wesley* (Lanham, Md.: University Press of America, 1987; reprint of 1964 ed.), p. 150.
19. Robert Southey, *The Life of Wesley; and Rise and Progress of Methodism*, vol. 2 (London: Longman, Brown, Green, and Longmans, 1846), p. 380.
20. Albert C. Outler, ed., *The Works of John Wesley*, Bicentennial ed., vols. 1–4, *The Sermons* (Nashville: Abingdon Press, 1984), 3:236.
21. Curnock, *Journal*, 7:436.

22. Outler, *Sermons,* 3:527, emphasis added.
23. Ward and Heitzenrater, *Journals and Diaries,* 23:235.
24. Outler, *Sermons,* 3:390.
25. Ibid., 3:391.
26. Ibid., 3:393, emphasis added.
27. Ibid., 1:519.
28. Ibid., 1:695, emphasis added.
29. Ibid.
30. Telford, *Letters,* 8:51.
31. Ibid., 8:52.
32. Ward and Heitzenrater, *Journals and Diaries,* 23:179-80.
33. Ibid., 23:287.
34. Curnock, *Journal,* 8:17.
35. Ibid., 8:35.
36. Outler, *Sermons,* 2:501.
37. Ibid., 3:152.
38. Telford, *Letters,* 7:231.
39. Outler, *Sermons,* 3:452.
40. Telford, *Letters,* 7:230.
41. Outler, *Sermons,* 4:121.
42. Ibid., 3:498.
43. Ibid., 3:130.
44. Ibid., 3:497.
45. Telford, *Letters,* 7:157.
46. Ibid., 7:95.
47. Outler, *Sermons,* 3:497-98.
48. Ibid., 4:35, emphasis added.

CHAPTER 10. GOD IS WITH US

1. Albert C. Outler, ed., *The Works of John Wesley,* vols. 1–4, *The Sermons* (Nashville: Abingdon Press, 1984), 4:146-47.
2. John Telford, ed., *The Letters of John Wesley, A.M.,* 8 vols. (London: Epworth Press, 1931), 8:218.
3. Ibid., 8:222.
4. Nehemiah Curnock, ed., *The Journal of the Rev. John Wesley, A.M.,* 8 vols. (London: Epworth Press, 1938), 8:93.
5. Telford, *Letters,* 8:234.
6. Outler, *Sermons,* 4:175.
7. Curnock, *Journal,* 8:102.
8. Telford, *Letters,* 7:76.
9. Ibid., 7:19.
10. Ibid., 7:33.
11. Ibid., 7:295.

12. Ibid., 7:322.

13. Albert C. Outler, ed., *The Works of John Wesley*, Bicentennial ed., vols. 1–4, *The Sermons* (Nashville: Abingdon Press, 1984), 2:169.

14. Telford, *Letters*, 8:238.

15. Ibid., 8:211.

16. Ibid., 8:224-25.

17. Ibid., 8:231.

18. Ibid., 8:265.

19. Ibid., 8:17.

20. Ibid., 8:23.

21. Ibid., 8:207.

22. Ibid., 8:199.

23. Curnock, *Journal*, 8:76.

24. Telford, *Letters*, 8:254.

25. Ibid., 8:257.

26. Ibid., 8:259.

27. Curnock, *Journal*, 8:138.

28. Ibid.

BIBLIOGRAPHY

PRIMARY SOURCES

Books

Baker, Frank, ed. *The Works of John Wesley*. Bicentennial Ed. Vol. 25, *Letters I*. Nashville: Abingdon Press, 1980.
————. *The Works of John Wesley*. Bicentennial Ed. Vol. 26, *Letters II*. Nashville: Abingdon Press, 1982.
Burwash, N., ed. *Wesley's Fifty-Two Standard Sermons*. Salem, Ohio: Schmul Publishing Co., 1967.

Cragg, Gerald R., ed. *The Works of John Wesley*. Bicentennial Ed. Vol. 11, *The Appeals to Men of Reason and Religion and Certain Related Open Letters*. Nashville: Abingdon Press, 1989.
Curnock, Nehemiah, ed. *The Journal of Rev. John Wesley*. 8 vols. London: Epworth Press, 1909-1916.

Davies, Rupert E., ed. *The Works of John Wesley*. Bicentennial Ed. Vol. 9, *The Methodist Societies, I: History, Nature, and Design*. Nashville: Abingdon Press, 1989.

Green, Richard. *The Works of John and Charles Wesley*. 2nd revised ed. New York: AMS Press, 1976. Reprint of the 1906 edition.

Hildebrandt, Franz, and Oliver Beckerlegge, eds. *The Works of John Wesley*. Bicentennial Ed. Vol. 7, *A Collection of Hymns for the Use of the People Called Methodists*. Nashville: Abingdon Press, 1983.

Jackson, Thomas, ed. *The Works of the Rev. John Wesley, M.A.* 14 vols. London: Wesleyan Methodist Book Room, 1829–1831. Reprinted Grand Rapids, Mich.: Baker Book House, 1978.
Jarboe, Betty M., comp. *Wesley Quotations: Excerpts from the Writings of John Wesley and Other Family Members*. Metuchen, N.J.: Scarecrow Press, 1990.

Outler, Albert C., ed. *John Wesley*. Library of Protestant Thought. New York: Oxford University Press, 1964.

———. *The Works of John Wesley*. Bicentennial Ed. Vols. 1–4, *The Sermons*. Nashville: Abingdon Press, 1984–1987.

Outler, Albert C., and Richard P. Heitzenrater, eds. *John Wesley's Sermons: An Anthology*. Nashville: Abingdon Press, 1991.

Telford, John, ed. *The Letters of the Rev. John Wesley, A.M.* 8 vols. London: Epworth Press, 1931.

Ward, W. Reginald, and Richard P. Heitzenrater, eds. *The Works of John Wesley*. Bicentennial Ed. Vols. 18–23, *Journals and Diaries I–VI*. Nashville: Abingdon Press, 1988–1995.

Wesley, John. *Explanatory Notes upon the New Testament*. London: William Bowyer, 1755. Most recent reprint, Grand Rapids, Mich.: Baker Book House, 1987.

———. *Explanatory Notes upon the Old Testament*. 3 vols. Bristol: William Pine, 1765. Facsimile reprint, Salem, Ohio: Schmul Publishers, 1975.

———. *A Christian Library, Consisting of Extracts from and Abridgements of the Choicest Pieces of Practical Divinity Which Have Been Published in the English Tongue*. 30 vols. London: T. Blanshard, 1819–1827

———. *A Plain Account of Christian Perfection*. London: Epworth Press. Philadelphia: Trinity Press International, 1990.

SECONDARY SOURCES

Books

Abelove, Henry. *The Evangelist of Desire: John Wesley and the Methodists*. Stanford, Calif.: Stanford University Press, 1990.

Ayling, Stanley. *John Wesley*. New York: William Collins Publishers, 1979; Abingdon, 1981.

Bready, J. Wesley. *This Freedom—Whence?* Winona Lake, Ind.: Light and Life Press, 1958.

Church, Leslie. *Knight of the Burning Heart*. London: Epworth Press, 1938.

Davey, Cyril. *John Wesley and the Methodists*. Nashville: Abingdon Press, 1985.

Dobree, Bonamy. *John Wesley*. Folcroft, Pa.: Folcroft Library Edition, 1974.

Edwards, Maldwyn. *Family Circle*. London: Epworth Press, 1961.

———. *John Wesley*. 4th ed. Madison, N.J.: General Commission on Archives, 1987.

Ethridge, Willie S. *Strange Fires: The True Story of John Wesley's Love Affair in Georgia*. Birmingham, Alabama: Vanguard, 1971.

Bibliography

Fitchett, W. H. *Wesley and His Century: A Study in Spiritual Forces*. London: Smith, Elder, & Co., 1906.

Green, V. H. H. *The Young Mr. Wesley*. New York: St. Martin's Press, 1961.
———. *John Wesley*. Lanham, Md.: University Press of America, 1987. Reprint of 1964 edition.

Heitzenrater, Richard P. *The Elusive Mr. Wesley*. 2 vols. Nashville: Abingdon Press, 1984.
———. *Wesley and the People Called Methodists*. Nashville: Abingdon Press, 1995.
Hulley, Leonard D. *Wesley: A Plain Man for Plain People*. Westville, South Africa: Methodist Church of South Africa, 1987.

Jackson, Thomas, ed., *The Journals of Rev. Charles Wesley*. 2 Vols. (London: John Mason, 1849; Grand Rapids, Mich.: Baker Book House, 1980).

Lee, Umphrey. *The Lord's Horseman: John Wesley the Man*. New York: Abingdon Press, 1928.
Lipsky, Abram. *John Wesley: A Portrait*. New York: AMS Press, 1928.
Lunn, Arnold. *John Wesley*. New York: Dial Press, 1929.

McConnell, Francis J. *John Wesley*. Nashville/New York: Abingdon-Cokesbury Press, 1939.
McNeer, May, and Lynd Ward. *John Wesley*. Nashville/New York: Abingdon Press, 1957.
Miller, Basil. *John Wesley*. Minneapolis, Minn.: Bethany House, 1969.

Overton, J. H. *John Wesley*. London: Methuen and Co., 1891.

Piette, Maximin. *John Wesley in the Evolution of Protestantism*. London: Sheed and Ward, 1938.
Pollock, John. *John Wesley*. Oxford, England: Lion Publishing, 1989.
Pool, Thomas E. *John Wesley the Soul Winner*. Salem, Ohio: Schmul Publishing Co., n.d.
Pudney, John. *John Wesley and His World*. New York: Charles Scribner's Sons, 1978.

Rack, Henry D. *Reasonable Enthusiast: John Wesley and the Rise of Methodism*. 2nd ed. Nashville: Abingdon Press, 1993.
Rattenbury, J. Ernest. *Wesley's Legacy to the World: Six Studies in the Permanent Values of the Evangelical Revival*. London: Epworth Press, 1928.
Rogal, Samuel J. *John and Charles Wesley*. New York: Macmillan, 1983.

Schmidt, Martin. *The Young Wesley: Missionary and Theologian of Missions*. London: Epworth Press, 1958.

————. *John Wesley: A Theological Biography.* 2 vols. Nashville: Abingdon Press, 1962–1973.

Slaatte, Howard. *Fire in the Brand: An Introduction to the Creative Work and Theology of John Wesley.* Lanham, Md.: University Press of America, 1983.

Snell, F. J. *Wesley and Methodism.* New York: Scribner, 1900.

Snyder, Howard A. *The Radical Wesley: Pattern for Church Renewal.* Grand Rapids, Mich.: Zondervan, 1987.

Southey, Robert. *The Life of Wesley; and Rise and Progress of Methodism.* 2 Vols. London: Longman, Brown, Green, and Longmans, 1846.

Telford, John. *The Life of John Wesley.* London: Wesleyan Methodist Book Room, 1899.

Tuttle, Robert G., Jr. *John Wesley: His Life and Theology.* Grand Rapids, Mich.: Zondervan, 1982.

Tyerman, Luke L. *The Life and Times of the Rev. John Wesley, M.A.* 3 Vols. New York: Burt Franklin, 1872.

Vickers, John. *John Wesley.* Fort Washington, Pa.: Christian Literature Crusade, 1977.

Vulliamy, C. E. *John Wesley.* Westwood, N.J.: Barbour and Co., 1985.

Watson, Richard. *The Life of Rev. John Wesley.* New York: Hoyt & Co., 1831.

Wood, A. Skevington. *The Burning Heart: John Wesley, Evangelist.* Minneapolis, Minn.: Bethany House, 1978.

Articles

Baker, Frank. "The Real John Wesley." *Methodist History* 12 (July 1974): 183-97.

————. "Investigating Wesley Family Traditions." *Methodist History* 26, no. 3 (April 1988): 154-62.

Bassett, Paul M. "Finding the Real John Wesley." *Christianity Today* 28, no. 16 (November 9, 1984): 86-88.

Collins, Kenneth J. "John Wesley's Correspondence with His Father." *Methodist History* 26, no. 1 (October 1987): 15-26.

————. "John Wesley's Relationship with His Wife as Revealed in His Correspondence." *Methodist History* 32, no. 1 (October 1993): 4-18.

Drakeford, John W. "How Growing Old Looks from Within: A Study of John Wesley's Perception of the Aging Process Revealed in His Journal's 'Birthday Reflections.'" *Journal of Religion and Aging* 1, no. 2 (Winter 1984): 39-51.

Edwards, M. "Reluctant Lover: John Wesley as Suitor." *Methodist History* 12 (January 1974): 46-62.

Harland, H. Gordon. "John Wesley." *Touchstone: Heritage and Theology in a New Age* 2, no. 3 (October 1984): 5-17.

Maser, Frederick E. "John Wesley's Only Marriage [with reply by Frank Baker, pp. 42-45]." *Methodist History* 16 (October 1977): 33-41.
———. "Things You've Really Wanted to Know About the Wesleys." *Methodist History* 29, no. 2 (January 1991): 119-21.

Pembroke, Neil F. "From Self-Doubt to Assurance: The Psychological Roots of John Wesley's Early Spiritual Development." *Journal of Psychology and Christianity* 13 (Fall 1994): 242-53.

Rogal, Samuel J. "John Wesley's Daily Routine." *Methodist History* 8 (October 1974): 41-51.

Smith, Warren Thomas. "The Wesleys in Georgia: An Evaluation." *The Journal of the Interdenominational Theological Center* 6 (Spring 1979): 157-67.

Turner, John M. "John Wesley: Theologian for the People." *Journal of United Reform Church History Society* 3 (1986): 320-28.

Wallace, Charles. "Simple and Recollected: John Wesley's Life-style." *Religion in Life* 46 (Summer 1977): 198-212.

Yrigoyen, Charles, Jr. "John Wesley—200th Anniversary Studies." Methodist History 29, no. 2 (January 1991): 63-121.

INDEX

SCRIPTURES